CBSE Term II 2022

Psychology

Class XI

- Complete Theory Covering NCERT
- Case Based Questions
- Short/Long Answer Type Questions
- 3 Practice Papers with Explanations

Authors
Farah Sultan
Kuhulika Sharma

CBSE Term II
2022

ARIHANT PRAKASHAN (School Division Series)

© **Publisher**

No part of this publication may be re-produced, stored in a retrieval system or by any means, electronic, mechanical, photocopying, recording, scanning, web or otherwise without the written permission of the publisher. Arihant has obtained all the information in this book from the sources believed to be reliable and true. However, Arihant or its editors or authors or illustrators don't take any responsibility for the absolute accuracy of any information published and the damage or loss suffered thereupon.

All disputes subject to Meerut (UP) jurisdiction only.

ॐ **Administrative & Production Offices**

Regd. Office

'Ramchhaya' 4577/15, Agarwal Road, Darya Ganj, New Delhi -110002
Tele: 011- 47630600, 43518550

ॐ **Head Office**

Kalindi, TP Nagar, Meerut (UP) - 250002, Tel: 0121-7156203, 7156204

ॐ **Sales & Support Offices**

Agra, Ahmedabad, Bengaluru, Bareilly, Chennai, Delhi, Guwahati, Hyderabad, Jaipur, Jhansi, Kolkata, Lucknow, Nagpur & Pune.

ॐ **ISBN :** 978-93-25796-86-7

ॐ **PRICE :** ₹125.00

PO No : TXT-XX-XXXXXXX-X-XX

Published by Arihant Publications (India) Ltd.

For further information about the books published by Arihant, log on to www.arihantbooks.com or e-mail at info@arihantbooks.com

Follow us on   

Contents

Watch Free Learning Videos

Subscribe **arihant** YouTube Channel

- ☑ Video Solutions of CBSE Sample Papers
- ☑ Chapterwise Important MCQs
- ☑ CBSE Updates

Syllabus CBSE Term II Class XI

Units	Topics	Periods	Marks
IV	Human Development	16	09
V	Sensory, Attentional and Perceptual Processes	12	08
VI	Learning	17	10
VII	Human Memory	15	08
	Total	**60**	**35**

UNIT - IV Human Development   16 Periods / 9 Marks

The topics in this unit are:
1. Introduction
2. Meaning of Development
   * Life-Span Perspective on Development
3. Factors Influencing Development
4. Context of Development
5. Overview of Developmental Stages
   * Prenatal Stage
   * Infancy
   * Childhood
   * Challenges of Adolescence
   * Adulthood and Old Age

UNIT - V Sensory, Attentional and Perceptual Processes   12 Periods / 8 Marks

The topics in this unit are:
1. Introduction
2. Knowing the world
3. Nature and varieties of Stimulus
4. Sense Modalities
5. Attentional Processes
   * Selective Attention
   * Sustained Attention
6. Perceptual Processes
   * Processing Approaches in Perception

7. The Perceiver
8. Principles of Perceptual Organisation
9. Perception of Space, Depth and Distance
    * Monocular Cues and Binocular Cues
10. Perceptual Constancies
11. Illusions
12. Socio-Cultural Influences on Perception

UNIT - VI   **Learning**   17 Periods / 10 Marks

The topics in this unit are:
1. Introduction
2. Nature of Learning
3. Paradigms of Learning
4. Classical Conditioning
    * Determinants of Classical Conditioning
5. Operant/Instrumental Conditioning
    * Determinants of Operant Conditioning
6. Key Learning Processes
7. Observational Learning
8. Cognitive Learning
9. Verbal Learning
10. Skill Learning
11. Factors Facilitating Learning
12. Learning Disabilities

UNIT - VI   **Human Memory**   15 Periods / 8 Marks

The topics in this unit are:
1. Introduction
2. Nature of Memory
3. Information Processing Approach: The Stage Model
4. Memory Systems: Sensory, Short-term and Long-term Memories
5. Levels of Processing
6. Types of Long-term Memory
    * Declarative and Procedural; Episodic and Semantic
7. Memory as a Constructive Process
8. Nature and Causes of Forgetting
    * Forgetting due to Trace Decay, Interference and Retrieval Failure
9. Enhancing Memory
    * Mnemonics using Images and Organisation

CBSE Circular

Acad - 51/2021, 05 July 2021

Exam Scheme Term I & II

केन्द्रीय माध्यमिक शिक्षा बोर्ड
(शिक्षा मंत्रालय, भारत सरकार के अधीन एक स्वायत संगठन)

CENTRAL BOARD OF SECONDARY EDUCATION
(An Autonomous Organisation under the Ministryof Education, Govt. of India)

Special Scheme for 2021-22

A. Academic session to be divided into 2 Terms with approximately 50% syllabus in each term:

The syllabus for the Academic session 2021-22 will be divided into 2 terms by following a systematic approach by looking into the interconnectivity of concepts and topics by the Subject Experts and the Board will conduct examinations at the end of each term on the basis of the bifurcated syllabus. This is done to increase the probability of having a Board conducted classes X and XII examinations at the end of the academic session.

B. The syllabus for the Board examination 2021-22 will be rationalized similar to that of the last academic session to be notified in July 2021. For academic transactions, however, schools will follow the curriculum and syllabus released by the Board vide Circular no. F.1001/CBSE-Acad/Curriculum/2021 dated 31 March 2021. Schools will also use alternative academic calendar and inputs from the NCERT on transacting the curriculum.

C. Efforts will be made to make Internal Assessment/ Practical/ Project work more credible and valid as per the guidelines and Moderation Policy to be announced by the Board to ensure fair distribution of marks.

Details of Curriculum Transaction

- Schools will continue teaching in distance mode till the authorities permit in-person mode of teaching in schools.

- **Classes IX-X: Internal Assessment** (throughout the year-irrespective of Term I and II) would include the *3 periodic tests, student enrichment, portfolio and practical work/ speaking listening activities/ project.*

- **Classes XI-XII: Internal Assessment** (throughout the year-irrespective of Term I and II) would include end of topic or unit tests/ exploratory activities/ practicals/ projects.

- Schools would create a student profile for all assessment undertaken over the year and retain the evidences in digital format.

- CBSE will facilitate schools to upload marks of Internal Assessment on the CBSE IT platform.

- Guidelines for Internal Assessment for all subjects will also be released along with the rationalized term wise divided syllabus for the session 2021-22.The Board would also provide additional resources like sample assessments, question banks, teacher training etc. for more reliable and valid internal assessments.

केन्द्रीय माध्यमिक शिक्षा बोर्ड
(शिक्षा मंत्रालय, भारत सरकार के अधीन एक स्वायत संगठन)
CENTRAL BOARD OF SECONDARY EDUCATION
(An Autonomous Organisation under the Ministryof Education, Govt. of India)

Term I Examinations:

- At the end of the first term, the Board will organize **Term I Examination** in a flexible schedule to be conducted between November-December 2021 with a window period of 4-8 weeks for schools situated in different parts of country and abroad. Dates for conduct of examinations will be notified subsequently.

- The Question Paper will have Multiple Choice Questions (MCQ) including case-based MCQs and MCQs on assertion-reasoning type. Duration of test will be **90 minutes** and it will cover only the rationalized syllabus of **Term I only** (i.e. approx. 50% of the entire syllabus).

- Question Papers will be sent by the CBSE to schools along with marking scheme.

- The exams will be conducted under the supervision of the External Center Superintendents and Observers appointed by CBSE.

- The responses of students will be captured on OMR sheets which, after scanning may be directly uploaded at CBSE portal or alternatively may be evaluated and marks obtained will be uploaded by the school on the very same day. The final direction in this regard will be conveyed to schools by the Examination Unit of the Board.

- Marks of the **Term I** Examination will contribute to the final overall score of students.

Term II Examination/ Year-end Examination:

- At the end of the second term, the Board would organize **Term II or Year-end Examination** based on the rationalized syllabus of Term II only (i.e. approximately 50% of the entire syllabus).

- This examination would be held around **March-April 2022** at the examination centres fixed by the Board.

- The paper will be of **2 hours duration** and have questions of different formats (case-based/ situation based, open ended- short answer/ long answer type).

- In case the situation is not conducive for normal descriptive examination **a 90 minute MCQ based exam** will be conducted at the end of the Term II also.

- Marks of the Term II Examination would contribute to the final overall score.

6. **Assessment / Examination as per different situations**

A. **In case the situation of the pandemic improves and students are able to come to schools or centres for taking the exams.**

Board would conduct Term I and Term II examinations at schools/centres and the theory marks will be distributed equally between the two exams.

B. **In case the situation of the pandemic forces complete closure of schools during November-December 2021, but Term II exams are held at schools or centres.**

Term I MCQ based examination would be done by students online/offline from home - in this case, the weightage of this exam for the final score would be reduced, and weightage of Term II exams will be increased for declaration of final result.

C. **In case the situation of the pandemic forces complete closure of schools during March-April 2022, but Term I exams are held at schools or centres.**

Results would be based on the performance of students on Term I MCQ based examination and internal assessments. The weightage of marks of Term I examination conducted by the Board will be increased to provide year end results of candidates.

D. **In case the situation of the pandemic forces complete closure of schools and Board conducted Term I and II exams are taken by the candidates from home in the session 2021-22.**

Results would be computed on the basis of the Internal Assessment/Practical/Project Work and Theory marks of Term-I and II exams taken by the candidate from home in Class X / XII subject to the moderation or other measures to ensure validity and reliability of the assessment.

In all the above cases, data analysis of marks of students will be undertaken to ensure the integrity of internal assessments and home based exams.

Dr. Joseph Emmanuel
Director (Academics)

Human Development

In this Chapter...

Introduction

From birth onwards changes of various kinds take place in an individual's life, which continue even during old age. Over a span of time, a human grows and develops, learns to communicate, walk, count, and read and write. She/he also learns to distinguish between right and wrong. She/he makes friends, goes through puberty, gets married, rears children, and grows old. Even though we differ from each other, we share many commonalities. Most of us learn to walk by the first year and talk by the second year. The key developmental processes and changes taking place in major periods during the life-span: prenatal, infancy, childhood, adolescence, adulthood, and old age.

Meaning of Development

Development is the pattern of progressive, orderly and predictable changes that begin at conception (fertilisation) and continue throughout life. Development mostly involves changes—both growth and decline in human life span and observed during old age. It is influenced by interlinked **biological**, **cognitive** and **socio-emotional** processes.

The role of **cognitive processes** in development related to mental activities associated with the processes of knowing and experiencing, such as thought, perception, attention, problem solving, etc.

Socio-emotional processes refer to changes in an individual's interactions with other people, changes in emotions and in personality. These influence human development. It is important to note that biological, cognitive and socio-emotional processes are interwoven. These processes influence changes in the development of the individual as a whole through the human life-span.

Life-Span Perspective on Development

The study of development according to the Life-Span Perspective (LSP) includes the following assumptions

(i) Development is life long process i.e. it takes place across all age groups starting from conception to old age. It includes both gains and losses, which interact in dynamic (change in one aspect goes with changes in others) ways throughout the life-span.

(ii) The various processes of human development i.e. biological, cognitive, and socio-emotional are mixed together in the development of a person throughout the life-span.

(iii) Development is multi-directional. Some dimensions or components of a given dimension of development may increase, while others may decrease.

(iv) Development is highly modifiable within person. This modifiability varies among individuals. This means skills and abilities can be improved or developed throughout the life-span.

(*v*) Development is influenced by historical conditions. For example, the career orientation of school students today is very different from those students who were in schools 50 years ago.

(*vi*) Development is concerned with a number of disciplines like psychology, anthropology, sociology and neuro-sciences. They study human development and try to provide answers to development throughout the life-span.

(*vii*) An individual responds and acts on contexts, which include what was inherited, the physical environment, social, historical and cultural contexts. For example, life events in everyone's life are not the same, e.g. death of a parent, earthquake, flood, etc. These affect the course of one's life as also the positive influences such as winning an award or getting a good job. People keep on changing with changing contexts.

Growth, Development, Maturation and Evolution

Growth refers to an increase in the size of body parts or of the organism as a whole. It can be measured or quantified, for example, growth in height, weight, etc.

Development is a process by which an individual grows and changes throughout the life cycle. The term development applies to the changes that have a direction and hold definite relationship with what precedes it, and in turn, will determine what will come after.

All changes which occur as a result of development are not of the same kind. Thus, changes in size (physical growth), changes in proportion (child to adult), changes in features (disappearance of baby teeth), and acquiring new features are varied in their pace and scope level.

Maturation refers to the changes that follow an orderly sequence and are largely dictated by the genetic blueprint which produces commonalities in our growth and development. For example, most children can sit without support by 7 months of age, stand with support by 8 months and walk by one year.

Evolution refers to species-specific changes. Natural selection is an evolutionary process that favours individuals or a species that are best adapted to survive and reproduce. The evolutionary changes are passed from one generation to the next within a species. Emergence of human beings from great apes took about 14 million years. It has been estimated that the 'Homo sapiens' came into existence only about 50,000 years ago.

Factors Influencing Development

People differ with respect to physical as well as psychological characteristics. Despite these variations no one can be mistaken for any other species.

It is due to the interaction of heredity and environment which make us to be different from each other. Both **genetic** and **environmental** factors influence development. These are discussed as follows

Genetic Factors

Genetic transmission is very complex. Most characteristics present in us are combinations of larger number of genes. It is also impossible to possess all the characteristics by our genetic structure.

Genes provide a distinct blueprint and timetable for the development of an individual. Genes do not exist in isolation and development occurs within the context of an individual's environment.

The **principles of heredity** explain the mechanism for transmission of characteristics by every species from one generation to the next with the help of genetic code. The genetic code causes a child to develop in a particular way. Due to human genetic code, a fertilised human egg grows into a human baby and cannot grow into an elephant, a bird or a mouse.

Genotype is known as the actual genetic material or a person's genetic heritage. However, not all of this genetic material is apparent or distinctly identifiable in our observable characteristics.

Phenotype is the way in which an individual's genotype is expressed in observable and measurable characteristics. It includes physical traits such as height, weight, eye and skin colour and many of the psychological characteristics such as intelligence, creativity and personality.

The observable characteristics of an individual are the result of the interaction between the person's inherited traits and the environment.

Environmental Factors

Environmental factors also influence development through their interaction with genetic factors. Genes set the limit and within that limit the environment influences development. Genes also play an important role in determining the type of environment their children will encounter.

Sandra Scarr (1992) believes that the environment which is provided by parents for their children depends to some extent on their own genetic predisposition (susceptibility).

For example, if parents are intelligent and are good readers they would provide children with books to read. The outcome of this could be that their children would become good readers who enjoy reading. But children themselves choose certain environments based on their genotype. These interactions with environment keep changing from infancy through adolescence.

Context of Development

Development always takes place in a particular socio- cultural context. Transition during one's lifetime such as entering school, becoming an adolescent, finding jobs, marrying, having children, retirement, etc., all are joint functions of the biological changes and changing in one's environments. The environment can change or alter during any time of the individual's lifespan.

Two different contextual views of development are discussed as follows

Bronfenbrenner's Model of Development

Urie Bronfenbrenner's view is that a child's development is significantly affected by the complex world that envelops her/him. His contextual view of development emphasises the role of environmental factors in the development of an individual. These are as follows

- **Microsystem** This is the first level of development which includes all the things where the child immediately/directly comes in contact with the family, peers, teachers and neighbourhood.
- **Mesosystem** It consists of relations between these contexts family, peers, teachers and neighbourhood. For example, the relation of parents with the teachers and view of parents about adolescent's friends, etc. are experience which influence an individual's relationships with others.
- **Exosystem** It includes events in social settings where the child does not participate directly but they influence the childs' experiences in the immediate context.
  For example, the transfer of father or mother may cause tension among the parents which might affect the interactions with the child or the general amenities available to the child like quality of schooling, libraries, medical care, means of entertainment, etc.

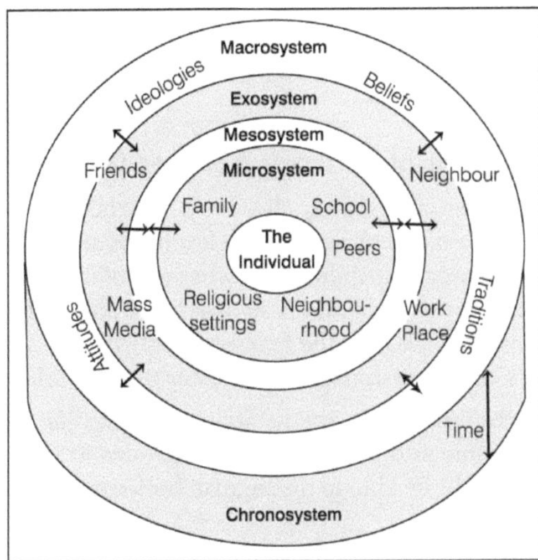

Bronfenbrenner's Contextual View of Development

- **Macrosystem** It includes the culture in which the individual lives.
- **Chronosystem** It involves events in the individual's life course and socio-historical circumstances of the time such as divorce of parents or parents' economic setback and their effect on the child.

Durganand Sinha's Model of Development

Durganand Sinha (1977) has presented an ecological model for understanding the development of children in Indian context.

Ecology of the child could be viewed in terms of two concentric layers which are as follows

(i) **Upper Layer** The most visible upper layer constitute the following ecological factors

- Home, its conditions in terms of overcrowding, space available to each member, toys, technological devices used, etc.
- Nature and quality of schooling and facilities to which the child is exposed.
- Nature of interactions and activities undertaken with peer groups from childhood onwards.

These factors do not operate independently but constantly interact with one another.

(ii) **Surrounding Layer** This layer constantly influence the upper layer factors. However, these influences are not always clearly visible. The elements of the surrounding layer of ecology constitute the following

- General geographical environment which includes space and facilities for play. Other activities available outside the home including general congestion of the locality and density of population.
- Institutional setting provided by caste, class and other factors.
- General facilities available to the child like drinking water, electricity, means of entertainment and so on.

The ecological environment can change or alter during any time of the individual's life span.

Therefore, to understand differences in the functioning of an individual, it is important to see the individual in the context of her/his experiences.

Overview of Developmental Stages

Development is commonly described in terms of periods or stages. For example, a person moves from stage of adolescence to stage of adulthood. Developmental stages are assumed to be temporary and are often characterised by a dominant feature or a leading characteristic, which gives each period its uniqueness.

During a particular stage, individual progresses towards an assumed goal which may be a state or ability that she/he must achieve in the same order as other persons before progressing to the next stage in the sequence. Certain patterns of behaviour and certain skills are learned more easily and successfully during certain stages which become the social expectations of that stage of development. They are known as **developmental tasks**.

Different stages of development and their main features are described as follows

Prenatal Stage

The period from conception to birth is known as the **prenatal period**. It lasts for about 40 weeks. Genetic blueprint guides our development during the prenatal period and after birth. Besides genetic and environmental factors, prenatal development is also affected by maternal characteristics, which include mother's age, nutrition and emotional state. Disease or infection carried by the mother can adversely affect prenatal development.

For example, **rubella** (German measles), **genital herpes** and **Human Immunodeficiency Virus** (HIV) are believed to cause genetic problems in the newborn.

Teratogens is another source of threat to prenatal development. They are environmental agents that cause deviations in normal development that can lead to serious abnormalities or death. Common teratogens include drugs, radiations and pollution. The effects of these are as follows

- Intake of **drugs** (marijuana, heroin, cocaine, etc), alcohol, tobacco, etc by women during pregnancy may have harmful effects on the foetus and increase the frequency of **congenital abnormalities**[1].
- **Radiations** (such as X-rays) and certain chemicals near industrial areas can cause permanent change in the genes.
- **Environmental pollutants** and toxic wastes like carbon monoxide, mercury and lead are also sources of danger to the unborn child.

Infancy Stage

The period just after birth to two years is marked as infancy. Just before birth the newborns have almost all brain cells. After birth, brain develops rapidly as the neural connections among the cells develop at a fast rate.

The activities needed to sustain life functions are present in the newborn i.e. he/she breathes, sucks, swallows and discharges the bodily wastes. During infancy motor development, development of **sensory abilities**, **cognitive development** and **socio-emotional development** take place.

The newborns in their first week of life are able to indicate what direction a sound coming from, can distinguish their mother's voice from the voices of other women can imitate simple gesture like tongue protrusion and mouth opening.

Motor Development During Infancy

Reflexes[2] govern the movement of newborns. These are automatic, built-in responses to stimuli. They are genetically-carried survival mechanisms and are the building blocks for subsequent motor development. Before the newborns have had the opportunity to learn, reflexes act as adaptive mechanisms.

Some reflexes like coughing, blinking and yawning present in the newborn continue throughout their lives. Other disappear as the brain functions mature and voluntary control over behaviour starts developing.

As the infant grows, the muscles and nervous system mature which lead to the development of finer skills. Basic physical (motor) skills include holding and reaching for objects, sitting, crawling, walking and running. The sequence of physical (motor) development is universal with minor exceptions.

Some Major Reflexes in the Newborn

Reflex	Description	Developmental Course
Rooting	Turnings the head and opening the mouth when touched on the cheek.	Disappears between 3 and 6 months
Moro	If there is a loud noise, the baby will throw her/his arms outward while arching her/his back, and then bring the arms together as if grasping something.	Disappears in 6 to 7 months (although reaction to loud noises is permanent)
Grasp	When a finger or some other object is pressed against the baby's palm the baby's fingers close around it.	Disappears in 3 to 4 months; replaced by voluntary grasping
Babinski	When the bottom of the baby's foot is stroked, the toes fan out and then curl.	Disappears in 8 to 12 months

Development of Sensory Abilities During Infancy

Infants can hear immediately after birth. Newborn can recognise their mother's voice just a few hours after birth and have other sensory capabilities. Newborns prefer to look at some stimuli rather than others such as faces, although these preferences changes over the first few months of life. The newborn's vision is estimated to be lower than the adult vision.

By 6 months it improves and by about the first year, **vision** is almost the same as that of an adult. It is a current view that newborns might be able to distinguish between red and white

---

1 **Congenital Abnormalities** An inherited medical condition that occurs at or before birth.
2 **Reflexes** It is an involuntary or automatic action that our body does in responses to something without your thinking about it.

colours but in general they are colour deficient and full colour vision develops by 3 months of age. Newborns respond to touch and they can even feel pain. Both smell and taste capacities are also present in the newborn.

Cognitive Development During Infancy

The child during infancy experiences the world through senses and interactions with objects i.e. through looking, hearing, touching, mouthing and grasping. The newborn lives in the present. If something is out of sight, it is out of mind of children at the stage. For example, if a person hides the toy in front of the child with which the child has been playing, the young infant would react as if nothing has happened, i.e. s/he will not search for the toy.

Children at this stage do not go beyond their immediate sensory experience i.e. lack object permanence (the awareness that the objects continue to exist when not perceived). Gradually by 8 months of age, the child starts pursuing the object partially covered in her/his presence. The basis of verbal communication seems to be present in infants. Vocalisation begins with the infant's babbling, sometime between 3 to 6 months of age.

Jean Piaget emphasis that children actively construct their understanding of the world. Information does not simply enter their minds from the environment.

As children grow, additional information is acquired and they adapt their thinking to include new ideas, as this improves their understanding of the world. Piaget believed that a child's mind passes through a series of stages of thought from infancy to adolescence.

Each stage is characterised by a distinct way of thinking and is age related. It is important to remember that it is the different way of thinking which makes one stage more advanced than the other and not the amount of information.

Piaget's Stages of Cognitive Development

Stage	Approximate Age	Characteristics
Sensorimotor	0-2 years	Infant explores the world by coordinating sensory experiences with physical actions.
Preoperational	2-7 years	Children use symbols to represent words, ideas and image: object permanence is established: the child cannot coordinate different physical attributes of an object.
Concrete operational	7-11 years	The child can reason logically about concrete events and classify objects into different sets. Is able to perform reversible mental operations on representa- tions of objects.
Formal operational	11-15 years	The adolescent can apply logic more abstractly: hypothetical thinking develops.

Socio-Emotional Development during Infancy

An infant starts preferring familiar faces and responds to parent's presence by cooing and gurgling (babbling). They become more energetic by 6 to 8 months of age and start showing a preference for their mother's company.

When frightened by a new face or when separated from their mother, they cry or show distress. On being reunited with the parent or care giver they reciprocate with smiles or hugs. The close emotional bond of affection that develops between infants and their parents (care givers) is called **attachment**.

In a classic study by **Harlow and Harlow** (1962), baby monkeys were separated from their mothers approximately 8 hours after birth. In this study, the baby monkeys were placed in experimental chambers and reared for 6 months by surrogate (substitute) mothers, one made of wire and the other of cloth. Half the baby monkeys were fed by the wire mother and half by the cloth mother.

It was observed in the study that the baby monkeys showed a preference for the cloth mother and spent a lot more time with her. This study clearly states that providing food was not crucial for attachment but contact-comfort is important. It is all about comfort due to which young children have strong attachment to a favourite toy or blanket, though it is not their mother, yet provides them comfort. When they grow up, they abandon these objects.

Human babies also form an attachment with their parents or care givers who consistently and appropriately reciprocate their signals of love and affection.

Effects of Responsive and Sensitive Parenting on Infant

According to **Erik Erikson** (1968), the first year of life is the key time for the development of attachment. It represents the stage of developing trust or mistrust. Effects of responsive and sensitive parenting on Infant are given below

A sense of trust is built on a feeling of physical comfort which builds an expectation of the world as a secure and good place. An infant's sense of trust is developed by responsive and sensitive parenting.

If the parents are sensitive, affectionate and accepting, it provides the infant a strong base to explore the environment. Such infants are likely to develop a secure attachment.

If the parents are insensitive and show dissatisfaction and find fault with the child, it can lead to creating feelings of self-doubt in the child.

Securely attached infants respond positively when picked up more freely and play whereas insecurely attached infants feel anxious when separated and cry due to fear and get upset.

Childhood Stage

Childhood is the stage between infancy and adolescence i.e. 3-10 years. The child's growth slows down during early childhood as compared to infancy. The **child develops physically**, gains height and weight, learns to walk, run, jump and play. In this stage, the child's world expands from the parents to the family and adults near home and at school. The child also begins to acquire the concepts of good and bad i.e. develops a sense of morality. During childhood, children have increased physical capacities, can perform tasks independently, can set goals and meet adult expectations.

Physical Development During Childhood

During this stage, the brain and the head grow more rapidly than any other part of the body. The growth and development of the brain are important as they help in the maturation of children's abilities, such as eye-hand coordination, holding a pencil and attempts made at writing.

During middle and late childhood years, children increase significantly in size and strength. Increase in weight is mainly due to increase in the size of the skeletal and muscular systems, as well as size of some body organs. Early development follows two principles. They are as follows

(i) Development proceeds **cephalocaudally** i.e. from the cephalic or head region to the caudal or tail region. Children gain control over the upper part of the body before the lower part. This is why, the infant's head is proportionately larger than her/his body during early infancy.

(ii) Growth proceeds from the centre of body and moves towards the extremities or more distal regions called the **proximodistal** trend i.e. children gain control over their upper body before their extremities. Initially infants reach for objects by turning their entire body, gradually they extend their arms to reach for things.

These changes are the result of a maturing nervous system and not because of any limitation since even visually impaired children show the same sequence. As children grow older, they look slimmer as the trunk part of their bodies lengthens and body fat decreases.

Motor Development During Childhood

Gross motor skills during the early childhood years involve the use of arms and legs and moving around with confidence and more purposefully in the environment. Fine motor skills i.e. finger skill and eye-hand coordination improve substantially during early childhood. During these years, the child's preference for left or right hand also develops.

Major Accomplishments in Gross and Fine Motor Skills

Age in Years	Gross Motor Skills	Fine Motor Skills
3 Years	Hopping, jumping, running	Build blocks, pick objects with forefinger and thumb
4 Years	Climb up and downstairs with one foot on each step	Fit jigsaw puzzle precisely
5 Years	Run hard, enjoy races	Hand, arm and body all coordinate with eye movement

Cognitive Development During Childhood

The increasing maturation of the brain along with opportunities to experience the world contribute to development of children's cognitive abilities. The child's ability to acquire the concept of object permanence enables him/her to use mental symbols to represent objects.

However, the child at this stage lacks the ability that allows her/him to do mentally what was done physically before. Cognitive development in early childhood focuses on Piaget's stage of preoperational thought.

The child gains the ability to mentally represent an object that is not physically present e.g. children draw designs/figures to represent people, trees, dog, house, etc. The ability of the child to engage in symbolic thought helps to expand her/his mental world.

Egocentrism During Childhood

In this stage, children see the world only in terms of their own selves and are not able to appreciate others' point of view.

Children because of egocentrism (self-focus), engage in animism (philosophical) thinking that all things are living, like oneself. As children grow and are approximately between 4 and 7 years of age they develop curiosity and ask questions about the things happening in surrounding. Piaget called this the stage of **intuitive thought**.

Another feature of thought during preoperational stage is characterised by children having a tendency for **centration**, i.e., focusing on a single characteristic or feature for understanding an event.

For example, a child may insist on drinking a big glass of juice preferring a tall narrow glass to short broad one, even though both might be holding the same amount of juice.

Concrete Operations During Childhood

As the child grows and is approximately between 7 and 11 years of age (the period of middle and late childhood) intuitive thought is replaced by **logical thought**. This is the stage of concrete operational thought, which is made up of operation i.e. mental actions that allows the child to do mentally what was done physically before.

Concrete operations are also mental actions that are reversible. In a well-known test, the child is presented with two identical balls of clay. One ball is rolled by the experimenter into a long thin strip and the other ball remains in its original shape.

On being asked which has more clay, the child of 7 or 8 years, would answer that, both have the same amount of clay. This is because the child imagines the ball rolled into thin strip and then into a ball, that means she is able to imagine reversible mental action on concrete/real objects.

Concrete operations allow the child to focus on different characteristics and not focus on one aspect of the object which also results in the decline of her/his egocentrism. Thinking becomes more flexible and children can think about alternatives when solving problems, or mentally retrace their steps if required.

Socio-Emotional Development during Childhood

The important dimensions of children's socio- emotional development are the self, gender and moral development. The child due to socialisation has developed a sense of who she/he is and whom she/he wants to be identified with. The developing sense of independence makes children do things in their own way.

According to **Erikson**, the way parents respond to their self-initiated activities leads to developing a sense of initiative or sense of guilt. For example, giving freedom and opportunities for play like cycling, running, skating, etc., and answering children's question will create a sense of support for the initiative taken.

In contrast, if they are made to feel that their questions are useless and games played by them are stupid, the children are likely to develop feelings of guilt over self-initiated activities, which may continue through the children's later life also.

Self-understanding in early childhood is limited to defining oneself through physical characteristics; Such as : I am tall, she has black hair, I am a girl, etc. During middle and late childhood, the child is likely to define oneself through internal characteristics such as, I am smart, I feel proud when teachers assign me responsibility in school.

In addition to defining oneself through psychological characteristics, children's self-descriptions also include social aspects of self, such as references to social groups.

Children's self-understanding also includes social comparison. Children are likely to think about what they can do or cannot do in comparison with others. For example, I got more marks than Atul or I can run faster than others in the class. The developmental shift leads to establishing one's differences from others as an individual.

Gender and Sex Roles

A gender role is a set of expectations that prescribes how females and males should think, act and feel. Parents and peers are important influences on gender socialisation especially in the early years of development. Through rewards and punishments, parents induce in children gender appropriate and inappropriate behaviours.

Parents restrict school-aged girls more than they restrict school-aged boys, and assign boys and girls different types of chores. Media, including cartoons and commercials are known to perpetuate gender stereotypes.

Once children learn the role of male or female, they organise their world on the basis of gender also. Children's attention and behaviour are guided by an internal motivation to conform to gender based socio-cultural standards and stereotypes. Children also actively socialise themselves according to the gender mores of their culture.

Once they have internalised gender standards, they begin to expect gender appropriate behaviour from themselves. Young boys may refuse to wear feminine clothes in a fancy dress competition. When playing house (ghar-ghar), girls may refuse to play the father's role.

The 'gender typing' occurs when individuals are ready to encode and organise information along the lines of what is considered appropriate or typical for males and females in a society.

Moral Development During Childhood

Another important aspect of the child's development is learning to differentiate between the rightness or wrongness of human acts. The way children come to distinguish right from wrong, to feel guilty, to put themselves in other people's position and to help others when they are in trouble, are all components of moral development.

According to **Lawrence Kohlberg**, just as children pass through the various stages of cognitive development, they pass through the various stages of age related moral development. According to him, children approach thinking about right and wrong differently at different ages. The young child, i.e. before 9 years of age, thinks in terms of external authority. According to her/him actions are wrong because she/he is punished and right because she/he is rewarded.

As the child grows, i.e. by early adolescence, she/he develops moral reasoning through set of rules of others, such as parents or laws of the society. These rules are accepted by the children as their own. These are internalised in order to be virtuous and to win approval from others (not to avoid punishment). Children view rules as absolute guidelines which should be followed.

Moral thinking in childhood is relatively inflexible. As children grow, they gradually develop a personal moral code. By the end of childhood a more gradual growth rate enables the child to develop skills of coordination and balance. Language develops and the child can reason logically. Socially the child has become more involved in social systems, such as family and peer group.

Adolescence

The term adolescence derives from the Latin word *adolescere,* meaning **to grow into maturity**. It is the transitional period in a person's life between childhood and adulthood. Adolescence is commonly defined as the stage of life that begins at the onset of puberty, when sexual maturity or the ability to reproduce is attained. It is a period of rapid change, both biologically and psychologically.

Though the physical changes that take place during this stage are universal, the social and psychological dimensions of the adolescent's experiences depend on the cultural context.

For example, in cultures where the adolescent years are viewed as problematic or confusing, the adolescent will have very different experiences from someone who is in a culture, where adolescent years are viewed as beginning of adult behaviour and therefore, undertaking responsible tasks. Although most societies have at least a brief period of adolescents, it is not universal across cultures.

Challenges of Adolescence

Some challenges of Adolescence are given below

Physical Development During Adolescence

Adolescence is characterised by dramatic physical changes in both, growth rate and sexual characteristics. Puberty is not a sudden event, it is part of a gradual process. The main features of physical development in adolescence are

- The hormones released during puberty result in the development of primary and secondary sexual characteristics. The primary sex characteristics include those directly related to reproduction and the secondary sex characteristics include features or signs of achieving sexual maturity.
- Pubertal changes in boys are marked by acceleration in growth, facial hair and changes in voice. In girls, rapid growth in height usually begins about two years before menarche, the onset of menstruation.
- The **growth spurt** generally begins at the age of 12 or 13 for boys and at the age of 10 or 11 for girls. It is normal to have variations in the pubertal sequence.

  For example, among two boys (or two girls) of same chronological age, one may complete pubertal sequence before the other has begun it. Both genetics and environment play a part in this. For example, identical twins reach menarche closer in time than do fraternal twins.

Psychological Development During Adolescence

Around puberty adolescents show an increase in interest in members of the opposite sex and in sexual matters and a new awareness of sexual feelings develops. This is caused by factors such as individual's awareness of the biological changes taking place and the emphasis placed on sexuality by peers, parents and society.

Even then, many adolescents lack adequate knowledge or have misconceptions about sex and sexuality. Sex is a topic parents find difficult to discuss with children, so adolescents tend to become secretive about sexual concerns which make exchange of information and communication difficult.

The concern over adolescent sexuality has become intense in recent times because of the risk of AIDS (Acquired Immunodeficiency Syndrome) and other sexually transmitted diseases. The development of a **sexual identity** defines the sexual orientation and guides sexual behaviour. It becomes an important developmental task for adolescents. Adolescents are preoccupied with there liking and develop individual images about their look. Another important developmental tasks during adolescence is accepting one's physical self/maturity.

Adolescents need to develop a realistic image of their physical appearance, which is acceptable to them. It is important to keep in mind that puberty also involves cognitive and social changes along with physical changes.

Cognitive Developments During Adolescence

During adolescence, thoughts become more abstract, logical, and idealistic. Adolescents become more capable of examining their own thoughts, others' thoughts and what others are thinking about them. Developing logical and reasoning ability of adolescent gives them a new level of cognitive and social awareness.

As per Piaget's cognitive development theory Formal operational thought appears between the age of 11 and 15. During this stage, adolescent's thinking expands beyond actual concrete experiences and becomes idealistic.

Adolescents begin to think about ideal characteristics for themselves and others and compare themselves and others with these ideal standards.

Development of Logical and Moral Thinking

Adolescent thinking becomes more systematic in solving problems as they think of possible courses of action, why something is happening the way it is and systematically seek solutions. Piaget called this type of logical thinking as **hypothetical deductive reasoning**.

Logical thought also influences the development of moral reasoning. Social rules are not considered as absolute standards and moral thinking shows some flexibility. The adolescent recognises alternative moral courses, explores options and then decides on a personal moral code which lends the possibility of adolescents not following society's norms if they conflict with personal code of ethics.

Adolescents' Egocentrism

Adolescents develop a special kind of egocentrism. According to **David Elkind**, there are two components of adolescents' egocentrism. They are as follows

(i) **Imaginary Audience** It is adolescent's belief that others are as preoccupied with them as they are about themselves. They imagine that people are always noticing them and are observing each and every behaviour of them which makes them extremely self-conscious.

(ii) **Personal Fable** It is part of the adolescents' egocentrism that involves their sense of uniqueness. Adolescents' sense of uniqueness makes them think that no one understands them or their feelings. To retain their sense of personal uniqueness they may weave stories filled with fantasy around them to create a world that is away from reality.

Identity Formation

Identity refers to distinguishing character or personality of an individual like her/his values, commitments and beliefs. The primary task of adolescence is to establish an identity separate from the parents. During adolescence a detachment process enables the individual to develop a personalised set of beliefs that are uniquely her or his own. In the process of achieving an identity the adolescent could experience conflict with parents and within herself or himself.

Those adolescents who can cope with the conflicting identities develop a new sense of self. Adolescents who are not able to cope with this identity crisis are confused. This **identity confusion**, according to Erikson can lead to individuals isolating themselves from peers and family or they may lose their identity in the crowd.

Adolescents on one hand, may desire independence but may also be afraid of it and show a great deal of dependence on their parents. Rapid fluctuations between self-confidence and insecurity are typical of this stage. Adolescents may at one time complain of being treated like 'a baby' whereas on other occasions they may seek comfort by depending on their parents.

Seeking an identity involves searching for continuity and sameness in oneself, greater responsibility and trying to get a clear sense of who one is i.e. an identity.

Factors Affecting Identity Formation

The formation of identity during adolescence is influenced by several factors such as

- Family relationships become less important as the adolescent spends more time outside the home and develops a strong need for peer support and acceptance. Increased interactions with peers provide them with opportunities for refining their social skills and trying out different social behaviours.

- Vocational commitment is another factor influencing adolescent identity formation. It includes question related to career, the ability to think about the future and to be able to set realistic and achievable goals. In some cultures, freedom is given to the young people to choose an occupation, whereas in certain other cultures the option of making this choice is not given to the children.

- Career counselling in schools offers information regarding appraisal of the students for various courses and jobs and provides guidance in making a decision about career choices.

Major Concerns During Adolescence

In this age, the issues like peer influence, new gained freedom, unresolved problems create difficulties for adolescent. Adolescents may face periods of uncertainty, loneliness, self-doubt, anxiety and concern about themselves and their future, they are also likely to experience excitement, joy and feelings of competence as they overcome the developmental challenges.

Some of the major challenges faced by adolescents are as follows

Delinquency

It refers to a **variety of behaviours**, such as socially unacceptable behaviour, legal offences, to criminal acts, etc. Examples include truancy, running away from home, stealing or burglary or acts of vandalism. Adolescents with delinquency and behavioural problems tend to have a negative self-identity, decreased trust and low level of achievement. Delinquency is often associated with low parental support, inappropriate discipline and family discord.

Often adolescents from communities characterised by poverty, unemployment, and having feelings of alienation from the middle class perform antisocial acts to gain attention and to be popular with their peers. However most delinquent children do not remain delinquent forever.

Change in the peer group, becoming more aware of their social responsibilities and developing feelings of selfworth, imitating positive behaviour of the role models, breaking negative attitudes and overcoming poor self-concept help in reduction of delinquent behaviour.

Substance Abuse

Adolescent years are especially vulnerable to **smoking**, **alcohol** and **drug abuse**. Some adolescents adopt smoking and drugs as a way of coping with stress which can interfere with the development of coping skills and responsible decision-making. The reasons for smoking and drug use could be as following

- Peer pressure and the adolescents' need to be accepted by the group.
- Desire to act more like adults.
- Feel a need to escape the pressure of school work.

The addictive powers of nicotine make it difficult to stop smoking. Adolescents who are more vulnerable to drugs, alcohol and nicotine use are impulsive, aggressive, anxious, depressive and unpredictable. They have low self-esteem and low expectation for achievement.

Drug use if continued long enough can lead to physiological dependency, i.e. addiction to drugs. Alcohol or nicotine may seriously endanger the rest of the adolescents' lives. Positive relationships with parents, peers, siblings and adults play an important role in preventing drug abuse.

Society for Theatre in Education Programme

In India, a successful anti-drug programme is the **Society for Theatre in Education Programme** in New Delhi. It uses street performances to entertain people between 13 to 25 years of age while teaching them how to say no to drugs.

The United Nations International Drug Control Programme (UNDCP) has chosen the programme as an example to be adopted by other non-governmental organisations in the region.

Eating Disorders

Anorexia nervosa and **bulimia** are two common eating disorders among adolescents. Anorexia nervosa and bulimia are primarily female disorders and are more common in urban families.

(i) **Anorexia nervosa** is an eating disorder that involves relentless pursuit of thinness through starvation. It is quite common to see adolescents eliminate certain foods from their diets or to eat slimming foods only. The media also projects thinness as the most desirable image and copying such fashionable image of thinness leads to anorexia nervosa.

(ii) **Bulimia** is another form of an eating disorder in which the individual follows a binge-and-purge eating pattern which means that the person goes on an eating binge, then purges by self-induced vomiting or using a laxative at times alternating it with fasting.

Adulthood

An adult is generally defined as someone who is **responsible, mature, self-supporting** and **well-integrated** into society. There is variation in developing these attributes, which suggests that there is a shift in timing when an individual becomes an adult or assumes adult roles. Some people take up jobs along with their college studies or may get married and not pursue their studies. Others may continue to live with their parents even after getting married and being financially independent. The assumption of adult roles is directed by an individual's social context. Adulthood is the best time for some of the most important life events i.e. marriage, job, having children. It might be quite different in different cultures but within a culture there is similarity in the course of adult development.

In early adulthood, two major tasks are i.e. exploring the possibilities for adult living and developing a stable life structure. It also represent the fresh phase of adult development.

Some of the challenges during adulthood are as follows

Career and Work

Earning a living, choosing an occupation and developing a career are important themes for people in their twenties and thirties. Entering work life is a challenging event in anyone's life. There are apprehensions regarding different adjustments, proving one's competence, performance, dealing with competition and coping with expectations both of the employers and oneself. It is also the beginning of new roles and responsibilities. Developing and evaluating a career becomes an important task of adulthood.

Marriage, Parenthood and Family

Adults have to make adjustments when entering in a marriage life. In addition to getting married, becoming a parent can be a difficult and stressful transition in young adults, even though it is usually accompanied by the feeling of love for the baby. Parenting experience is affected by different situations such as the number of children in the family, the availability of social support, and the happiness or unhappiness of the married couple.

Death of a spouse or divorce creates a family structure in which a single parent either the mother or the father has to take up the responsibility of the children.

In recent times, women are increasingly seeking employment outside the home thus creating another type of family in which both parents work. The stressors when both parents are working are quite the same as of a single working parent, namely, taking care of children, their schoolwork, illness and coping with workload at home and in the office, etc.

Despite the stresses associated with parenting, it provides a unique opportunity for growth and satisfaction and is perceived as a way of establishing concern and guiding the next generation.

Physical Changes During Adulthood

Physical change during middle ages are caused by maturational changes in the body. Though individuals may vary in the rate at which these changes occur, almost all middle-aged people notice gradual deterioration in some aspects of their physical functioning such as decline in vision, sensitivity to glare, hearing loss and changes in physical appearance e.g. (shine wrinkles, grey hair or thinning of hair, weight gain).

It is believed that some cognitive abilities decline with age while others do not. Decline in memory is more in tasks involving long-term memory than short-term memory.

For example, a middle-aged person can remember the telephone number immediately after she/he has heard it but may not remember it so efficiently after a few days. Memory tends to show greater decline, while wisdom may improve with age. It is to be noted that individual differences exist in intelligence at every age and as not all children are exceptional, neither do all adults show wisdom.

Old Age

Traditionally, the age of retirement was linked to old age. Some of the challenges, which the aged have to cope with include **retirement**, **widowhood**, **illness** or **death** in the family.

The experience of old age depends on the socio-economic conditions, availability of health care, attitude of people, expectations of society and the available support system. Work is most important during early adult years, then family becomes most important and in old age health becomes the most important issue in the person's life.

Clearly, successful ageing for much of our adult life focuses on how effective we are at work, how loving our relationships are in our family, how good our friendships are, how healthy we are and how cognitively fit we are.

Retirement from active vocational life is quite significant. Some people perceive retirement as a negative change. They consider it as a separation from an important source of satisfaction and self-esteem. Other view it as a shift in life with more time to pursue their own interests. It is seen that older adults who show openess to new experiences, achievement-oriented behaviour and prefer to keep busy are better adjusted.

Dependency

Older adults also need to adjust to changes in the family structure and new roles (grand parenting) that have to be learnt. Children usually are busy in their careers and families and may set up independent homes.

Older adults may depend on their children for financial support and to overcome their loneliness. In old age, **feeling of loss of energy** and **diminishing of health** and **financial** assets lead to insecurity and dependency.

The elderly tend to look towards others to lean on and to care for them. Indian culture favours dependency of elderly on their children, for old age needs caring. In fact, parents in most oriental cultures rear their children with the fond hope that they will care for them during old age. It is important to give the elderly a sense of security and belonging, a feeling that people care for them (especially in the time of crisis), and to remember that we all have to grow old one day.

Death

Although death is more likely to occur in late adulthood, death can come at any point in development. The deaths, especially of children and younger adults, are often perceived to be more tragic than those of others. In children and younger adults, death is more likely to occur because of accidents but in older adults it is more likely to occur because of chronic disease.

The death of a spouse is usually seen as the most difficult loss. Those left behind after the death of their partner suffer deep grief, cope with loneliness, depression, financial loss and are also at risk of many health related problems. People in different cultures view death differently. In the Gond culture in our country, it is believed that death is caused by magic and demon. In the Tanala culture of Madagascar, natural forces are thought to cause death.

Chapter Practice

Objective Questions

• Multiple Choice Questions

1. _________ is the pattern of progressive, orderly and predictable changes that begin at conception and continue throughout life.
(a) Growth (b) Development
(c) Maturation (d) Evolution

Ans. (b) Development is the pattern of progressive, orderly and predictable changes that begin at conception and continue throughout life.

2. _________ is known as the actual genetic material or a person's genetic heritage.
(a) Phenotype (b) Heredity (c) Genes (d) Genotype

Ans. (d) Genotype is known as the actual genetic material or a person's gentic heritage.

3. Which of these factors According to Bronfenbrenner, Model of Development, consists of relations between these contexts family, peers, teachers and neighbourhood?
(a) Mesosystem (b) Exosystem
(c) Macrosystem (d) Chronosystem

Ans. (a) According to Bronfenbrenner, Mesosystem consists of two or more microsystems. Home and school can be part of a child's mesosystem.

4. _________ can be affected by maternal malnutrition, maternal drug use and some maternal illnesses.
(a) Motor development (b) Prenatal development
(c) Sensory Development (d) Post-natal development

Ans. (b) Prenatal development can be affected by maternal malnutrition, maternal drug use and other maternal illness.

5. According to Jean Piaget, the period of infancy is marked by which of these cognitive development stages?
(a) Formal operational stage (b) Preoperational stage
(c) Concrete operational stage (d) Sensorimotor stage

Ans. (d) According to Jean Piaget, the period of infancy is marked by the sensorimotor cognitive development stage. The first stage of cognitive development according to Piaget, is the Sensorimotor stage which is from 0-2 years of age.

6. Rituraj is hopping, running and jumping in lobby of his house. Which type of skills does it exemplify?
(a) Fine motor skills (b) Gross motor skills
(c) Major motor skills (d) Development motor skills

Ans. (b) Hopping, running and jumping exemplify Gross Motor Skills.

7. Which of these following statements about the Life-span perspective are correct?
(i) Development is a fairly short process i.e, it starts at conception and completes as one reaches adolescence.
(ii) Development is multi-directional. Some dimensions or components of a given dimension of development may increase, while others may decrease.
(iii) Development is not influenced by historical conditions.
(iv) The various processes of human development, i.e biological, cognitive, socio-emotional are interlinked.
Choose the correct option
(a) (i) & (iv) (b) (ii) & (iii)
(c) (i) & (iii) (d) (ii) & (iv)

Ans. (d) Biological, cognitive and socio-emotional factors are the various processes of human development. Human development is multi-directional. One's performance in some areas increases with age and decreases in other aspects.

8. Consider the following statements and determine which of the two are correct?
(i) Gross Motor Skills: Hopping, jumping, running
(ii) Fine Motor Skills: Run hard, enjoy races
(iii) Gross Motor Skills: Fit jigsaw puzzle precisely
(iv) Fine Motor Skills : Build blocks, pick objects with forefinger and thumb
Choose the correct option
(a) (i) & (iv) (b) (i) & (ii) (c) (ii) & (iii) (d) (iii) & (iv)

Ans. (a) Hopping, jumping and running are the activities which are the examples of Gross Motor Skills and Build Blocks, Pick Objects with forefinger and skills thumb are the examples of Fine Motor Skills.

9. The role of __________ in development relates to mental activities associated with the processes of knowing and experiencing, such as thought, perception, attention, problem solving, etc.

(a) socio-emotional processes

(b) cognitive processes

(c) developmental processes

(d) growth processes

Ans. (b) The role of cognitive processes in development relates to mental activities associated with the process of knowing and experiencing, such as thought, perception, attention, problem solving.

10. Itika, who is 15 years old, thinks about what an ideal parent is like and compares her parents with the ideal standards. She also thinks about the new-found ideal standards parents should adopt. According to Piaget, which stage of cognitive development does this example represent?

(a) Sensorimotor (b) Formal operational

(c) Concrete operational (d) Preoperational

Ans. (b) According to Piaget it is Formal operational stage from 11-15 years of the age. At this stage, the adolescent is capable of engaging in more logical and abstract thinking. During this stage, he or she can engage in hypothetical situations.

11. According to David Elkind, these are the two components of adolescents' egocentrism.

(i) Imaginary audience (ii) Hypothetical-thinking

(iii) Personal fable (iv) Identity formation

Choose the correct option

(a) (i) & (ii) (b) (ii) & (iv)

(c) (i) & (iii) (d) (iii) & (iv)

Ans. (c) Two components of egocentrism are imaginary audience and personal fable.

Imaginary audience means that the adolescent believes that others pay more attention to them than it is true and secondly, personal fable, refers to adolescent's belief in his or her own sense of uniqueness.

12. Pawan who is 13 years old enters the school library and instantly thinks that everyone is watching him. As per David Elkind, Pawan is most likely experiencing which of the following?

(a) Hypothetical deductive reasoning

(b) Personal fable

(c) Perspective taking

(d) Imaginary audience

Ans. (d) Pawan is most likely experience Imaginary audience. It is an aspect of egocentrism which refers to the tendency of adolescents to believe that people pay more attention to them than it is true. They think that everyone is focusing on them.

13. Raghav is 16 years old and has fallen into the habit of smoking every time he feels stressed out. He first tried a cigarette when he became part of a group of video gamers. He then gradually got into the habit of smoking more frequently and now smoking has become a coping mechanism.

He is suffering from which of the following psychological problems?

(a) Eating disorder

(b) Anxiety disorder

(c) Substance-abuse disorder

(d) Mood disorder

Ans. (c) Raghav is suffering from Substance-abuse disorders which involve excessive consumption of a substance which leads to psychological and physical harm. The person addicted to a substance is not able to stay without consuming it.

14. Charu belongs to the Gond culture of India. There is a long-standing belief in her culture that death is caused by __________.

(a) natural forces (b) biological reasons

(c) magic and demons (d) accidents

Ans. (c) There is a long standing belief in her culture that death is caused by magic and demons.

15. Which of the following is true about Harry Harlow's experiment on monkeys?

(i) Baby monkeys were separated from their mothers approximately 8 hours after birth.

(ii) The baby monkeys were placed in an open jungle and were reared real monkeys.

(iii) The baby monkeys were placed in experimental chambers and reared for 6 months by surrogate (substitute) "mothers", one made of wire and the other of cloth.

(iv) The baby monkeys showed a preference for the wire mother and felt safe around her.

Choose the correct option

(a) (i) & (ii) (b) (ii) & (iv)

(c) (i) & (iii) (d) (iii) & (iv)

Ans. (c) In Harry Harlow's experiment, baby monkeys were separated from their mothers approx 8 hours after birth. They were exposed to two surrogate mothers, in which one was made of wire and the other made of cloth. The wire mother had milk while the cloth mother did not. The baby monkeys preferred the cloth mother for comfort and safety. Thus option (c) is the correct answer.

• Assertion-Reasoning MCQs

Directions (Q. Nos. 1-4) *Each of these questions contains two statements, Assertion (A) and Reason (R). Each of these questions also has four alternative choices, any one of which is the correct answer. You have to select one of the codes (a), (b), (c) and (d) given below.*

(a) Both A and R are true and R is the correct explanation of A

(b) Both A and R are true, but R is not the correct explanation of A

(c) A is true, but R is false

(d) A is false, but R is true

1. Assertion (A) It has been seen that wisdom tends to increase as one ages, while physical abilities decline with time.

Reason (R) This is because development is multi-directional.

Ans. (a) Both A and R are true and R is the correct explanation of A.

Development takes place in different aspects such as physical, psychological, and cognitive. Some abilities tend to improve with time, while others decline. This is because development is a multi-directional process.

2. Assertion (A) Most children can sit without support by 7 months of age, stand with support by 8 months and walk by one year.

Reason (R) Evolution refers to species-specific changes.

Ans. (c) Here, Assertion (A) is true, but Reason (R) is false. A seven month old infant can sit without support which was not possible when he/she was 2-month-old. The reason why a child can do that is because of maturation which refers to aging and growth which takes place in a gradual manner.

3. Assertion (A) If you hide the toy in front of a newborn child with which the child has been playing, he/she would react as if nothing has happened, i.e. s/he will not search for the toy.

Reason (R) According to Jean Piaget, an infant lacks object permanence.

Ans. (a) According to Jean Piaget, young infants lacks object permanence i.e. they are incapable of understanding that an object continues to exist even if it is out of sight. If you hide a toy infront of a child, he would not search for the same. Thus, Both Assertion (A) and Reason (R) are true and R is the correct explanation of A.

4. Assertion (A) A three years old child is likely to say "stone hurt me" after tripping on the road because of a stone lying on the road.

Reason (R) Egocentrism causes young children to engage in animism.

Ans. (a) According to Piaget, an aspect of egocentrism is animism which means that young children think that objects/non-living things also have life and therefore react to objects as they would to a real person/animal. Thus, Both Assertion (A) and Reason (R) are true and R is the correct explanation of A.

• Case Based MCQs

1. Read the case and answer the questions that follow.

Parker is a child psychologist who works on the theory of Jean Piaget. When he observes children of infancy stage he found different activities done by these infants. During his research work he observed that the child during infancy experiences the world through senses and interactions with objects i.e. through looking, hearing, touching, mouthing and grasping. The newborn lives in the present. If something is out of sight, it is out of the minds of children at this stage. For example, once Parker hid a toy in front of a child with which the child was playing. The young infant did react as if nothing had happened, i.e. she did not search for the toy. The the child assumed the toy did not exist. Parker recalls the theory of Jean Piaget that children at this stage, have lack object permanence i.e. the awareness that the objects continue to exist when not perceived. Gradually by 8 months of age, the child starts pursuing the object partially covered in her/his presence. As per this theory Vocalisation begins with the infant's babbling, sometime between 3 to 6 months of age. Jean Piaget stressed that children actively construct their understanding of the world. Information does not simply enter their minds from the environment. As children grow, additional information is acquired and they adapt their thinking to include new ideas, as this improves their understanding of the world.

(i) Parker works on which theory of child psychology?

(a) Social Construct theory

(b) Behavioural theory of B.F Skinner

(c) Cognitive theory of Jean Piaget

(d) Humanist theory of Carl Rogers

Ans. (c) Parker works on cognitive theory of Jean Piaget. Parker follows Piaget's theoretical fundamentals as a child psychologist.

(ii) In the theory of Jean Piaget, Parker observed which phenomenon during the infancy stage?

(a) Word Formation

(b) Usage of Correct Grammar

(c) Lack of Object Permanence

(d) All of the above

Ans. (c) Parker observed that the infant showed lack of object permanence which means that the child thought that an object stops existing if it is not in his or her sight.

(iii) As per the theory of Jean Piaget, vocalisation begins with the infant's babbling, sometime between the age of

(a) 0 to 3 months   (b) 3 to 6 months

(c) 6 to 7 months   (d) 9 to 11 months

Ans. (b) According to Piaget, it is between 3 to 6 months of age when the infant starts uttering things. Infant starts cooing and babbling around this time.

(iv) What is the correct definition of an object permanence?

(a) The ability to reach out and grab an object.

(b) The ability to name an object.

(c) The ability to know that not seeing an object does not mean it does not exist.

(d) The ability to know that the object has a specific function in the environment.

Ans. (c) Object permanence is the ability to know that not seeing an object does not mean it does not exist. Thus, option (c) is the correct answer.

(v) Infant explores the world by coordinating sensory experiences with __________.

(a) parent's actions

(b) physical action

(c) social interaction

(d) reward and punishment

Ans. (b) Sensorimotor is the stage where infant explores the world by coordinating sensory experiences with physical action.

(vi) The given case in passage is an example of which stages of cognitive development given by Piaget?

(a) Concrete operational   (b) Formal operational

(c) Sensorimotor   (d) Preoperational

Ans. (c) The case given in passage is an passage example of Sensorimotor.

PART 2

Subjective Questions

• Short Answer (SA) Type Questions

1. Discuss the genetic factors that influence development.

Ans. The genetic factors that influence development are as follows

- Genes provide a distinct blueprint and timetable for the development of an individual.
- The principles of heredity explain the mechanism for transmission of characteristics by every species from one generation to the next with the help of genetic code. It is because of the human genetic code that a fertilised human egg grows into a human baby and cannot grow into an elephant, a bird or a mouse.
- Genetic transmission is very complex. Most characteristics are combinations of larger number of genes.
- It is also impossible to possess all the characteristics by our genetic structure.

2. Discuss the environmental factors that influence development.

Ans. The environmental factors that influence development are as follows

- Genes set the limit and within that limit the environment influences development.
- Genes also play an important role in determining the type of environment their children will encounter.

- Sandra Scarr (1992) believes that the environment which is provided by parents for their children depends to some extent on their own genetic predisposition.
- Children themselves choose certain environments based on their genotype. These interactions with environment keep changing from infancy through adolescence. Environmental influences are as complex as the genes one inherit.

3. Differentiate between genotype and phenotype.

Ans. The difference between genotype and phenotype is given in the table as follows

Genotype	Phenotype
Genotype is the actual genetic material or a person's genetic makeup.	Phenotypes are a set of observable characteristics of an individual.
Genotype includes collection of genes responsible for the various genetic traits of a person.	They are a result of the interaction of its genotype with the environment.
It simply indicates specifically to the genes, not to the traits.	Height, weight, eye and skin colour, intelligence and creativity are some examples of phenotype.
Not all genes have observable traits. Some can have observable results.	Some observable characteristics of an individual are the results of the interaction between the person's inherited traits and the environment.

4. What is ecology of the child? Explain the ecological factors that influence development.

Ans. Child ecology deals with the interaction of children with their environment in life including human relationships. Durganand Sinha has presented an ecological model for understanding the development of children in Indian context. Ecology of the child could be viewed in terms of two concentric layers. These are as follows

(i) **Upper Layer** The most important ecological factors influencing development of the child in the visible upper layer constitute the following

- Home, its conditions in terms of overcrowding, space available to each member, toys, technological devices used, etc.
- Nature and quality of schooling and facilities to which the child is exposed.
- Nature of interactions and activities undertaken with peer groups from childhood onwards.

(ii) **Surounding Layer** The elements of the surrounding layer of ecology constitute the following

- General geographical environment which includes space and facilities for play.
- Institutional setting provided by caste, class and other factors.
- General facilities available to the child like drinking water, electricity, means of entertainment and so on.

5. What are the effects of teratogens?

Ans. Teratogens are harmful for human body especially for foetus. Common teratogens include drugs, radiations, and pollution. The effects of teratogens are as follows

- Intake of drugs (marijuana, heroin, cocaine, etc), alcohol, tobacco, etc by women during pregnancy may have harmful effects on the foetus and increase the frequency of congenital abnormalities.
- Radiations (such as X-rays) and certain chemicals near industrial areas can cause permanent change in the genes.
- Environmental pollutants and toxic wastes like carbon monoxide, mercury and lead are also sources of danger to the unborn child.

6. Explain the development of sensory abilities in new borns.

Ans. The development of sensory abilities in new borns started just after birth. By 6 months it improves and by about the first year, vision is almost the same as that of an adult. They might be able to distinguish between red and white colours but in general they are colour deficient and full colour vision develops by 3 months of age.

Infants can hear immediately after birth. As the infant develops, proficiency at localising sound improves.

Newborns respond to touch and they can even feel pain. Both smell and taste capacities are also present in the newborn.

7. Describe briefly the development of child in the childhood stage.

Ans. The child develops physically, gains height and weight, learns to walk, runs, jumps and plays. Socially, the child's world expands from the parents to the family and adults near home and at school.

The child also begins to acquire the concepts of good and bad i.e. develops a sense of morality. During childhood, children have increased physical capacities, can perform tasks independently, can set goals and meet adult expectations. The increasing maturation of the brain along with opportunities to experience the world, contribute to development of children's cognitive abilities.

8. What is adolescence? Explain the concept of egocentrism.   (NCERT)

Ans. **Adolescence** is commonly defined as the stage of life that begins at the onset of puberty, when sexual maturity or the ability to reproduce is attained. It has been regarded as a period of rapid change, both biologically and psychologically.

Egocentrism Deals with self-focus. It is a viewpoint of the world that is centred upon the self. It hinders an appreciation of the viewpoint of others.

The egocentrism in adolescents comprises the following two elements

(i) **Imaginary Audience** It is adolescent's belief that others are as preoccupied with them as they are about themselves. They imagine that people are always noticing them and are observing each and every behaviour of them which makes them extremely self-conscious.

(ii) **Personal Fable** It is part of the adolescents' egocentrism that involves their sense of uniqueness. Adolescents' sense of uniqueness makes them think that no one understands them or their feelings.

9. "Adolescence is definitely a vulnerable period." Comment .

Ans. It is true that adolescence is definitely a vulnerable period. During adolescence, peer influence, new gained freedom and unresolved problems may create difficulties for youth. Conforming to peer pressure can be both positive and negative. Adolescents are often confronted with decisions regarding smoking, drugs, alcohol and breaking parental rules, etc.

These decisions are taken without much regard to the effect they can have. Adolescents may face periods of uncertainty, loneliness, self-doubt, anxiety and concern about themselves and their future. They are also likely to experience excitement, joy and feelings of competence as they overcome the develop- mental challenges.

10. What are major challenges faced by adolescents? Discuss the challenge of substance abuse.

Ans. Some major challenges faced by adolescents are delinquency, substance abuse and eating disorders.

Substance abuse It is the use of a drug (such as alcohol, smoking etc) in amounts or by methods which are harmful to the individual. It is also known as drug abuse.

Some adolescents take recourse to smoking and drugs as a way of coping with stress which can interfere with the development of coping skills and responsible decision-making. The reasons for smoking and drug use could be

- Peer pressure and the adolescents' need to be accepted by the group.
- Desire to act more like adults.
- Feel a need to escape the pressure of school work.

The addictive powers of nicotine make it difficult to stop smoking. Adolescents who are more vulnerable to drugs, alcohol and nicotine use are impulsive, aggressive, anxious, depressive, and unpredictable, have low self-esteem and low expectation for achievement.

Drug use if continued long enough can lead to physiological dependency, i.e. addiction to drugs, alcohol or nicotine may seriously jeopardise the rest of the adolescents' lives.

11. Explain eating disorders in adolescents.

Ans. Eating disorders are those psychological disorders that involve extreme disturbances in eating behaviour. These are two common eating disorders among adolescents namely Anorexia nervosa and Bulimia. These are discussed as follows

Anorexia nervosa is an eating disorder that involves relentless pursuit of thinness through starvation. It is quite common to see adolescents eliminate certain foods from their diets or to eat slimming foods only.

Bulimia is another form of an eating disorder in which the individual follows a binge-and- purge eating pattern.

The bulimic goes on an eating binge, then purges by self-induced vomiting or using a laxative at times alternating it with fasting.

12. "The myth of old age as an incapacitating is changing." Discuss the statement in context of old aged challenges.

Ans. Now people are living longer, age of retiring from work is changing and the cut-off point for the definition of 'old age' is moving upward.

Some of the challenges, which the aged have to cope with include retirement, widowhood, illness or death in the family. The image of old age is changing in certain ways. Now there are people who have crossed seventy years of age or so and are quite active, energetic and creative. They are competent and are therefore, valued by society in many walks of life. In particular, we have aged people in politics, literature, business, art and science.

Hence, the myth of old age as an incapacitating and therefore, frightening phase of life is changing.

13. Mansi is doing a research work on old age people. She finds that there are many challenges at this stage but the most common is dependency. Why dependency mostly affects the old age people?

Ans. Dependency is the common issue/challenge found among old age people. It is because old adults may depend on their children for financial support and to overcome their loneliness (after children have moved out). This might trigger-off feelings of hopelessness and depression in some people.

In old age feeling of loss of energy, and dwindling of health and financial assets, lead to insecurity and dependency. The elderly tend to look towards others to lean on and to care for them.

Indian culture favours dependency of elderly on their children, for old age needs caring. In fact, parents in most oriental cultures rear their children with the fond hope that they will care for them during old age.

It is important to give the elderly sense of security and belonging, a feeling that people care for them (especially in the time of crisis) and to remember that we all have to grow old one day.

14. How do socio-cultural factors influence development?

Ans. Following are the socio-cultural factors which influence the development of an individual

- Development is influenced by socio-cultural factors which provides social context to development.
- The various socio-cultural consequences that a child meets with are learnt by him/her. As a result a child develops such personality which is influenced by his/her experiences.
- Every person has different socio-cultural background which impacts his/her interaction with the rest of the society.
- During the developmental period of an individual his variable experiences are dependent upon their social and cultural background.
- These factors include the conditions at home, the quality of schooling and interaction with peer groups.
- Children who have unstable family environment find it hard to learn new things and make their own decisions. Children who are exposed to diverse experiences early in life develop a confident attitude and are more able to face challenges.

15. What are the factors affecting identity formation?

Ans. The formation of identity during adolescence is influenced by several factors such as

- Family relationships become less important as the adolescent spends more time outside the home and develops a strong need for peer support and acceptance. Increased interactions with peers provide them with opportunities for refining their social skills and trying out different social behaviours.

- Vocational commitment is another factor influencing adolescent identity formation. It includes question related to career, the ability to think about the future and to be able to set realistic and achievable goals. In some cultures, freedom is given to the young people to choose an occupation, whereas in certain other cultures the option of making this choice is not given to the children.

- Career counselling in schools offers information regarding appraisal of the students for various courses and jobs and provides guidance in making a decision about career choices.

16. Discuss the challenges faced by old aged people.

Ans. Some of the challenges, which the aged people have to cope with include the following

- Older adults may depend on their children for financial support and to overcome their loneliness. This might trigger-off feelings of hopelessness and depression in some people.

- In old age, feeling of loss of energy and diminishing of health and financial assets lead to insecurity and dependency.

- Retirement from active vocational life can also be a challenging and difficult experience for many older adults.

- The deaths, especially of children and younger adults, are often perceived to be more tragic than those of others.

- In children and younger adults, death is more likely to occur because of accidents but in older adults it is more likely to occur because of chronic disease.

- The death of a spouse is usually seen as the most difficult loss. Those left behind after the death of their partner suffer deep grief, cope with loneliness, depression, financial loss and are also at risk of many health related problems.

- As some may view it as a separation from an important source of satisfaction and self-esteem.

• Long Answer (LA) Type Questions

1. What are the assumptions which are included in the study of development according to the Life-Span Perspective?

Ans. The study of development according to the Life-Span Perspective (LSP) includes the following assumptions

- Development is life long process i.e. it takes place across all age groups starting from conception to old age. It includes both gains and losses, which interact in dynamic (change in one aspect goes with changes in others) ways throughout the life-span.

- The various processes of human development i.e. biological, cognitive, and socio-emotional are mixed together in the development of a person throughout the life-span.

- Development is multi-directional. Some dimensions or components of a given dimension of development may increase, while others may decrease.

- Development is highly modifiable within person. This modifiability varies among individuals. This means skills and abilities can be improved or developed throughout the life-span.

- Development is influenced by historical conditions. For example, the career orientation of school students today is very different from those students who were in schools 50 years ago.

- Development is concerned with a number of disciplines like psychology, anthropology, sociology and neuro-sciences. They study human development and try to provide answers to development throughout the life-span.

- An individual responds and acts on contexts, which include what was inherited, the physical environment, social, historical and cultural contexts.

2. Define Bronfenbrenner's Model of Development.

Ans. Urie Bronfenbrenner's view is that a child's development is significantly affected by the complex world that envelops her/him. His contextual view of development emphasises the role of environmental factors in the development of an individual. These are as follows

- **Microsystem** This is the first level of development which includes all the things where the child immediately/directly comes in contact with the family, peers, teachers and neighbourhood.

- **Mesosystem** It consists of relations between these contexts family, peers, teachers and neighbourhood. For example, the relation of parents with the teachers and view of parents about adolescent's friends, etc. are experience which influence an individual's relationships with others.

- **Exosystem** It includes events in social settings where the child does not participate directly but they influence the childs' experiences in the immediate context. For example, the transfer of father or mother may cause tension among the parents which might affect the interactions with the child or the general amenities available to the child like quality of schooling, libraries, medical care, means of entertainment, etc.

- **Macrosystem** It includes the culture in which the individual lives.
- **Chronosystem** It involves events in the individual's life course and socio-historical circumstances of the time such as divorce of parents or parents' economic setback and their effect on the child.

3. Explain Durganand Sinha's Model of Development.

Ans. Durganand Sinha (1977) has presented an ecological model for understanding the development of children in Indian context. Ecology of the child could be viewed in terms of two concentric layers which are as follows

(i) **Upper Layer** The most visible upper layer constitute the following ecological factors

- Home, its conditions in terms of overcrowding, space available to each member, toys, technological devices used, etc.
- Nature and quality of schooling and facilities to which the child is exposed.
- Nature of interactions and activities undertaken with peer groups from childhood onwards.

These factors do not operate independently but constantly interact with one another.

(ii) **Surrounding Layer** This layer constantly influence the upper layer factors. However, these influences are not always clearly visible. The elements of the surrounding layer of ecology constitute the following

- General geographical environment which includes space and facilities for play. Other activities available outside the home including general congestion of the locality and density of population.
- Institutional setting provided by caste, class and other factors.
- General facilities available to the child like drinking water, electricity, means of entertainment and so on.

4. Discuss about the concrete operations during childhood.

Ans. As the child grows and is approximately between 7 and 11 years of age (the period of middle and late childhood) intuitive thought is replaced by **logical thought**. This is the stage of concrete operational thought, which is made up of operation i.e. mental actions that allows the child to do mentally what was done physically before.

Concrete operations are also mental actions that are reversible. In a well-known test, the child is presented with two identical balls of clay. One ball is rolled by the experimenter into a long thin strip and the other ball remains in its original shape.

On being asked which has more clay, the child of 7 or 8 years, would answer that, both have the same amount of clay. This is because the child imagines the ball rolled into thin strip and then into a ball, that means she is able to imagine reversible mental action on concrete/real objects.

Concrete operations allow the child to focus on different characteristics and not focus on one aspect of the object which also results in the decline of her/his egocentrism. Thinking becomes more flexible and children can think about alternatives when solving problems, or mentally retrace their steps if required.

5. What is development? How is development different from growth and maturation? **(NCERT)**

Ans. Development is the pattern of progressive, orderly and predictable changes that begin at conception and continue to take place throughout an individual's life.

Differences between growth and development are as follows

Growth	Development
Growth refers to an increase in the size of body parts or of the organism as a whole.	Development refers to a larger process, which is in terms of growth and maturation both.
Growth is measurable and quantified.	Development is not always measurable and quantified.
Any change that does not lead to the decline in age is considered as growth.	The change that leads to decline such as in old age is also considered as development.

Differences between maturation and development are as follows

Maturation	Development
Maturation refers to the changes that follow an orderly sequence.	Development does not necessarily refer to orderly sequence.
Maturation is largely dictated by the genetic blueprint which produces commonalities in the growth.	Development needs not to be identified with genetic changes and growth.

6. Discuss the cognitive changes taking place in a developing child. **(NCERT)**

Ans. The cognitive changes take place during different stages of development in the life of a developing child. These are as follows

0-2 Years This is the age of sensori motors whereby, infant explores the world by coordinating sensory experiences with physical actions.

2-7 Years In this age, preoperational thinking begins and the child acquires the concept of object permanence that enables him/her to use mental symbols to represent objects. However, the child at this stage lacks the ability that allows her/him to do mentally what was done physically before. The child does not have the ability to judge or assume the consequences of actions before performing them. The child gains the ability to mentally represent an object that is not physically present e.g. children draw designs/ figures to represent people, trees, dog, house, etc. The ability of the child to engage in symbolic thought helps to expand her/his mental world.

7-11 Years This age is marked by the development of concrete operational thought.

As the child grows and is approximately between 7 and 11 years of age (the period of middle and late childhood) intuitive thought is replaced by **logical thought.** This is the stage of concrete operational thought, which is made up of operation i.e. mental actions that allows the child to do mentally what was done physically before.

11-15 Years The adolescents in this age develop formal operational thought, which leads to a hypothetical thinking and are able to apply logic abstractly. They also develop a special kind of egocentrism of imaginary audience and personal fable.

7. Attachment bonds formed in childhood years have long-term effects. Explain taking examples from daily life. **(NCERT)**

Ans. The close emotional bond of affection that develops between infants and their parents (care givers) is called attachment. Human babies form an attachment with their parents or care-givers who consistently and appropriately reciprocate to their signals of love and affection.

According to Erik Erikson (1968), the first year of life is the key time for the development of attachment. It represents the stage of developing trust or mistrust. A sense of trust is built on a feeling of physical comfort which builds an expectation of the world as a secure and good place.

An infant's sense of trust is developed by responsive and sensitive parenting. For example, if the parents are sensitive, affectionate and accepting, it provides the infant a strong base to explore the environment.

Such infants are likely to develop a secure attachment. On the other hand, if parents are insensitive and show dissatisfaction and find fault with the child, it can lead to creating feelings of self-doubt in the child.

It is seen in our daily life that securely attached infants respond positively when picked up, move freely and play whereas insecurely attached infants feel anxious when separated and cry due to fear and get upset. A close interactive relationship with warm and affectionate adults is a child's first step towards healthy development.

8. What are the factors influencing the formation of identity during adolescence? Support your answer with examples.

Ans. The formation of identity during adolescence is influenced by several factors. Some of these are explained as follows

- **Cultural Background** The cultural background and the level of their exposure the ideas and opinions of adolescents about the world around them. These factors fix the norms followed by them and hence, their cultural identity. For example, adolescent behaviour varies among Indian and American cultulres.
- **Family and Societal Values** Adolescents practice some values of society in which they live and these values shape their identity. For example, teenagers in European countries are conditioned to a materialistic society in contrast to young adults in Tibet who are more spiritually inclined.
- **Ethnic Background** In order to make their own identity adolescents distinguish themselves as members of their ethnic group. For example, expectations of teenage behaviour and responsibilities vary across different ethnicities and tribes.
- **Socio-economic Status** It is seen that the socio-economic background of an adolescent ensures the peer group and the extent of their accessibility to popular lifestyle choices that determine identity. For example, accessibility to expensive gadgets and branded clothing that are popular among teenagers are determined by their socio-economic background.
- **Vocational Commitment** Adolescents begin to think of their career as a component of their identity. For example, adolescents choose whether to study arts, or commerce.

9. Discuss the challenges of marriage, parenthood and family faced by adults.

Ans. The challenges of marriage, parenthood and family faced by adults are as follows

- Adults have to make adjustments when entering in a marriage life like, to knowing the other person if not known earlier, coping with each other's likes, dislikes, tastes and choices.
- If both the partners are working, adjustments are required regarding sharing and performing roles and responsibilities at home.
- In addition to getting married, becoming a parent can be a difficult and stressful transition in young adults, even though it is usually accompanied by the feeling of love for the baby.

- Parenting experience is affected by different situations such as the number of children in the family, the availability of social support, and the happiness or unhappiness of the married couple.
- Death of a spouse or divorce creates a family structure in which a single parent either the mother or the father has to take up the responsibility of the children.
- In recent times, women are increasingly seeking employment outside the home thus creating another type of family in which both parents work. The stressors when both parents are working are quite the same as of a single working parent, namely, taking care of children, their schoolwork, illness and coping with workload at home and in the office, etc.

• Case Based Questions

1. Read the passage and answer the following questions.

Sarah is a 4 years old girl, who lives with her parents, an elder brother, and grandparents. Sarah and her family belong to the Indian culture.

She is very close to her neighborhood aunt because she gives her cookies and chocolates every time she sees her.

She has recently started going to a play school. There she loves to interact with her teacher and other children. Everyday after school, Sarah's mother, before picking her up, talks to her teacher.

Recently, Sarah's father was asked to move to a different city because of the promotion he got at work. Now all of them have to relocate. This leaves her upset because she liked her neighbour and play school teacher as well as her friends.

(i) From the given passage, identify the microsystem, mesosystem, and exosystem given in Bronfenbrenner's theory.

Ans. Microsystem is the immediate environment of the individual. Sarah's microsystem includes her parents, siblings, neighborhood aunt, and play school teacher.

Mesosystem is the interaction between two or more microsystems. Mesosystem includes Sarah's parents' view of her playschool teacher.

Exosystem- Social factors affecting the child with which he/she is not directly associated. In this case, Sarah's father's transfer caused her to feel sad and upset denotes exosystem.

(ii) Briefly describe Urie Bronfenbrenner's contextual view of development.

Ans. Urie Bronfenbrenner's contextual view of development states the importance of environmental factors in the development of an individual. An individual's environment consists of a microsystem, mesosystem, exosystem, macrosystem, and chronosystem. According to this theory,

a child's development is heavily influenced and affected by the complex world which surrounds him/her.

(iii) What are chronosystems? Give examples.

Ans. Chronosystems include all the events and experiences in the individual's life course, and socio-historical circumstances of the time such as, divorce of parents or parents' economic issues, and their effect on the child.

2. Read the passage and answer the following questions.

This case is about three siblings. Avni is 1 year old. She is playing with a wooden block. She throws it on the ground to see it's sturdiness and then puts the block in her mouth to feel its texture and taste.

When her older brother hides the doll she was playing with, she forgets about it and acts surprised and happy when he shows the doll to her.

Avni's older brother Varun likes eating chocolate cake but his sister does not and he finds it difficult and annoying to know that she does not like what he likes. He also believes that the flowers growing in his garden talk to him and have feelings like him.

Gayatri is the oldest among the three and she finds it easy to engage in hypothetical situations and discusses the different outcomes/consequences of the same action. She also thinks about what being an ideal parent is like and compares her parents against those ideals.

(i) Identify the stages of cognitive development by Piaget to which all three Avni, Varun and Gayatri belong.

Ans. Avni is in the Sensorimotor stage (0-2 years), Varun is in the Concrete operational stage and Gayatri is in the formal operational stage.

(ii) Briefly describe the theory of cognitive development.

Ans. Jean Piaget asserted that as a child grows their cognitive abilities change and enhance. He stated that children actively construct their understanding of the world.

As children grow, additional information is acquired and they adapt their thinking to include new ideas, as this improves their understanding of the world.

He explained how this cognitive development occurs in different stages.

(iii) What is hypothetical deductive reasoning and who among the three in the story was able to display this skill?

Ans. Among the three, Gayatri possesses hypothetical deductive reasoning. According to Piaget, an adolescent gains the ability to engage in abstract and logical thinking. They are now capable of thinking about the various possible courses of action and why things happen the way they do.

3. Read the passage and answer the following questions.

This is a case of Ananya and her older sister Sravani, who recently turned 21 and is soon going to complete her graduation in Biology. Although, she is confused between taking a break after college to explore different cities and joining university for master's degree, as she plans to go into the research field. She thinks about moving out of home and living an independent life also.

Sravani is 28 and works as a writer for a company. She got recently engaged to a guy who she was in a relationship with for some time.

As the wedding day is coming closer, she started worrying and thinking about how married life can be, what being a parent means and so on. She also feels concerned about how she would manage career and married life.

(i) Identify and define the developmental stage to which Sravani and Ananya belong.

Ans. Saravani and Ananya are in the adulthood stage of life. Ananya is at a place where she is exploring what she wants to do in life and Sravani's concerns are related to marital responsibilities and challenges she might have to face after marriage.

(ii) What are the two main tasks in the given developmental stage and briefly describe them.

Ans. The two important tasks in adulthood are exploring the possibilities for adult living and developing a stable life structure. Career and marriage become two important areas of focus for adults in this stage. Adulthood involves concerns regarding earning a living, choosing an occupation, along with concerns regarding marriage and adjusting with another person.

(iii) In addition to the challenges mentioned in the passage, what other challenges do people in this developmental stage experience?

Ans. Challenges faced by people in the developmental stage are biological challenges, cognitive challenges, psychological challenges.

Chapter Test

Multiple Choice Questions

1. Which of the following is a component of egocentrism?
- (a) Imaginary audience
- (b) Personal fable
- (c) Both (a) and (b)
- (d) None of these

2. Adolescents who are more vulnerable to drugs, alcohol and nicotine use are
- (a) Impulsive
- (b) Personal fable
- (c) Anxious
- (d) None of these

3. The important dimensions of children's socio-emotional development are
- (a) Self
- (b) Gender
- (c) Moral
- (d) All of these

4. Which of the following factor influence the development of a human being?
- (a) Environmental
- (b) Genetic
- (c) Both (a) and (b)
- (d) None of these

Short Answer (SA) Type Questions

5. What do you mean by socio-emotional process?

6. Define phenotype.

7. Give some examples of delinquency.

8. What is anoxeria nervosa?

9. What is animism?

10. What is concrete operational thought?

11. What are the characteristics of adolescence?

12. Describe any two reflexes in the newborn.

13. What is chronosystem? How is it different from mesosystem and exosystem?

14. How does the environment affect development? Explain in brief.

15. Explain physical development that occurs in an adult.

Long Answer (LA) Type Questions

16. Describe with examples maturation and development.

17. Explain the factors that influence the formation of identity during adolescence.

18. Discuss duties of family members towards old aged.

Answers

1. (a)   **2.** (c)   **3.** (a)   **4.** (c)

CHAPTER 02

Sensory, Attentional and Perceptual Processes

In this Chapter...

Introduction

This chapter focuses on how our receptors collect a variety of information from the external and internal worlds. Some receptors are clearly observable (like eye and ear) and others are inside our body. They are not observable without the help of electrical or mechanical devices.

In this chapter, we will also discuss about the attention. Attention helps us to notice and register the information that our sense organs carry to us.

Knowing the World

The knowledge about various objects becomes possible with the help of our sense organs (e.g. eyes, ears). These organs collect information not only from the external world, but also from our own body.

In order to be registered, the objects and their qualities e.g. size, shape, colour must be able to draw our attention. The registered information must also be sent to the brain that constructs some meanings out of them.

Our knowledge of the world around us depends on three basic processes, called **sensation, attention** and **perception**. These processes are highly interrelated and hence considered as part of the process called **cognition**.

Nature and Varieties of Stimulus

The outside environment that surrounds us contains a wide variety of stimuli. There are different sense organs which allow us to see, hear, smell, taste and touch different stimuli. All these stimuli provide us with different kinds of information. We have a set of seven sense organs, which are known as sensory receptors or information gathering systems, because they gather information from different kinds of sources. Five sense organs namely **eyes**, **ears**, **nose**, **tongue** and **skin** collect information from outside world.

Eyes are responsible for vision, ears for hearing, nose for smell, tongue for taste and skin is responsible for the experiences of touch, warmth, cold and pain. Specialised receptors of warmth, cold and pain are found inside our skin.

Apart from these five external sense organs, we also have two **deep senses**. They are called kinesthetic and vestibular systems. They provide us information about our body position and movement of body parts related to each other.

With these seven sense organs, we register ten different varieties of stimuli. For example, you may notice whether a light is bright or dim, whether it is yellow, red, or green and so on.

Sense Modalities

The initial experience of a stimulus or an object registered by a particular sense organ is **called sensation**. It refers to a process through which we detect and encode a variety of physical stimuli.

Different sense organs deal with different purposes. Each sense organ is highly specialised for dealing with a particular kind of information. Hence, each one of them is known as a **sense modality**.

Functional Limitations of Sense Organs

Functional limitations of sense organs are as follows

- Our eyes cannot see things which are very dim or very bright.
- Our ears cannot hear very faint or very loud sounds.
- Human beings can only function within a limited range of stimulation.

Some other functional limitations of sense organ are discussed below

Absolute Threshold/Limen (AL)

A stimulus has to carry a minimum value or weight in order to get noticed. The minimum value of a stimulus required to activate a given sensory system is called **absolute threshold** or Absolute Limen (AL).

For example, if you add a granule of sugar to a glass of water, you may not experience any sweetness in that water. But if you go on adding sugar granules one after another, there will come a point when you will say that the water is now sweet. The minimum number of sugar granules required to say that the water is sweet will be the AL of sweetness.

It is important to note that at this point that the AL is not a fixed point; instead it varies considerably across individuals and situations depending on the people's organic conditions and their motivational states.

Difference Threshold/Limen (DL)

We see that it is not possible for us to notice all stimuli, it is also not possible to differentiate between all stimuli. There should be some minimum difference between the two stimuli in order to notice the difference. The smallest difference in the value of the two stimuli that is necessary to tell them that they are different is called **difference threshold** or **Difference Limen** (DL).

It can be understood by the sugar water experiment. The number of sugar granules added to the water to generate an experience of sweetness that is different from the previous sweetness on 50 per cent of the occasions will be called the DL of sweetness. Thus, difference threshold is the minimum amount of change in a physical stimulus that is capable of producing a sensation difference on 50 per cent of the trials.

Understanding Sensory Processes

A sense organ receives the stimulus and encodes it as an electrical impulse and in order to get noticed it must reach the higher brain centers. Any structural or functional defect or damage in the receptor organ and its neural pathway (the concerned brain area) may lead to a partial or complete loss of sensation.

Attentional Processes

The process through which certain stimuli are selected from a group of others is generally referred to as **attention**. Attention also refers to several other properties like **alertness**, **concentration** and **search**. Alertness refers to an individual's readiness to deal with stimuli that appear before her/him.

Concentration refers to focusing of awareness on certain specific objects while excluding others for the moment. For example, when we just look for a person among innumerable persons. This kind of activity requires some kind of effort on the part of people. Attention in this sense refers to **effort allocation**.

Attention has a focus as well as a fringe (outer part of an area). When the field of awareness is centered on a particular object or event, it is called focus or the focal point of attention. On the other hand, when the objects or events are away from the center of awareness and one is not very clear of them, they are said to be at the fringe of attention.

Divided Attention

When we can attend to two different things at the same time, it is called divided attention. In day-to-day life we attend to several things at the same time.

But, this becomes possible only with highly practiced activities, because they become almost automatic and require less attention to perform than new or slightly practised activities. Automatic processing has three main characteristics. These are as follows

- It occurs without intention.
- It takes place unconsciously.
- It involves very little or no thought processes.

Classification of Attention

Attention has been classified in a number of ways. A process-oriented view divides it into two types, namely **selective** and **sustained**.

Selective Attention

It is concerned mainly with the selection of a limited number of stimuli or objects from a large number of stimuli. Our perceptual system has a limited capacity to receive and process information. This means that it can deal only with a few stimuli at a given moment of time.

Factors Affecting Selective Attention

Several factors influence Selective Attention. These generally relate to the characteristics of stimuli and the characteristics of individuals. They are generally classified as external and internal factors. These are discussed as follows

(i) **External Factors** These are related to the features of stimuli. The size, intensity and motion of stimuli are important determinants of attention. Large, bright and moving stimuli easily catch our attention.

Stimuli, which are novel and moderately complex, also easily get into our focus. Rhythmic auditory stimuli are more readily attended than verbal narrations. Sudden and intense stimuli have a wonderful capacity to draw attention.

(ii) **Internal Factors** These lie within the individuals. These may be divided into two main categories. These are as follows

(a) **Motivational Factors** These are related to our biological or social needs. When we are hungry, we notice even a light smell of food. A student taking an examination is likely to focus on a teacher's instructions more than other students.

(b) **Cognitive Factors** These include factors like interest, attitude and preparatory set. Objects or events, which appear interesting are readily attended by individuals.

Similarly, we pay quick attention to certain objects or events to which we are favourably disposed. Preparatory set generates a mental state to act in a certain way and readiness of the individual to respond to one kind of stimuli and not to others.

Theories of Selective Attention

Different theories have been developed to explain the process of selective attention.

Some of the important among them are as follows

(i) **Filter Theory** This theory was developed by **Broadbent** in 1956. As per this theory, many stimuli simultaneously enter our receptors creating a kind of 'bottleneck' situation. Moving through the short-term memory system, they enter the selective filter, which allows only one stimulus to pass through for higher levels of processing.

Other stimuli are screened out at that moment of time. Thus, we become aware of only that stimulus, which gets access through the selective filter.

(ii) **Filter-Attenuation Theory** It was developed by **Triesman** in 1962 by modifying **Broadbent's** theory. As per this theory, stimuli not getting access to the selective filter at a given moment of time are not completely blocked. The filter only attenuates (weakens) their strength. Thus, some stimuli manage to escape through the selective filter to reach higher levels of processing.

It is indicated that personally relevant stimuli (like one's name in a collective dinner) can be noticed even at a very low level of sound. Such stimuli, even though fairly weak, may also generate response occasionally by slipping through the selective filter.

(iii) **Multimode Theory** It was developed by **Johnston** and **Heinz** in 1978. This theory believes that attention is a flexible system that allows selection of a stimulus over others at three stages.

These stages are as follows

- At the **first stage**, the sensory representations i.e. visual images of stimuli are constructed.
- At the **second stage**, the semantic i.e. meanings of words representations like names of objects are constructed.
- At the **third stage**, the sensory and semantic representations enter the consciousness.

It is also suggested that more processing requires more mental effort. When the messages are selected on the basis of first stage processing i.e. early selection, less mental effort is required than when the selection is based on the third stage processing i.e. late selection.

Sustained Attention

It is concerned with concentration. It refers to our ability to maintain attention on an object or event for longer durations. It is also known as **vigilance**. Sometimes people have to concentrate on a particular task for many hours.

Factors influencing Sustained Attention

Several factors which can facilitate or interfere an individual's performance on tasks of sustained attention are as follows

(i) **Sensory Modality** Performance is found to be superior when the stimuli (called signals) are auditory than when they are visual.

(ii) **Clarity of Stimuli** Intense and long lasting stimuli facilitate sustained attention and result in better performance.

(iii) **Temporal Uncertainty** When stimuli appear at regular intervals of time they are attended better than when they appear at irregular intervals.

(iv) **Spatial Uncertainty** Stimuli that appear at a fixed place are readily attended, whereas those that appear at random locations are difficult to attend.

Span of Attention

The number of objects one can attend to at a fraction of second is called span of attention or perceptual span. More specifically, the span of attention refers to the amount of information an observer can grasp from a complex array of stimuli at a single momentary exposure. This can be determined by the use of an instrument, called **tachistoscope**. On the basis of several experiments, Miller has reported that our span of attention differs within the limit of seven plus or minus two. This is popularly known as the magic number.

It means that at a time, people can attend to a set of five to seven numbers, which can be extended to nine or more under exceptional conditions. That is why motorbikes or cars are given a number plate that contains only four digit numbers with some alphabets. In case of violation of driving rules a traffic police can easily read and note these numbers along with the alphabets.

Attention Deficit Hyperactivity Disorder (ADHD)

ADHD is a very common behavioural disorder found among children of the primary school age. It is characterised by impulsivity, excessive motor activity and an inability to attend.

The disorder is more common among boys than girls. If not managed properly, the attention difficulties may continue into adolescence or adult years.

Difficulty in maintaining attention is the main feature of this disorder, which gets reflected in several other domains of the child.

For example, such children are highly distractible, they do not follow instructions, have difficulty in getting along with parents and are negatively viewed by their peers. They do poorly in school, and show difficulties in reading or learning basic subjects in schools in spite of the fact that there is no deficit in their intelligence.

Studies generally do not provide evidence for a biological basis of the disorder, whereas some relationship of the disorder with dietary factors particularly food colouring, has been documented.

On the other hand, social-psychological factors (e.g. home environment, family pathology) have been found to account for ADHD more reliably than other factors. Currently ADHD is considered to have multiple causes and effects.

Treatment of ADHD

Standard treatment for ADHD typically involves the following

- A drug, called **Ritalin** is widely used, which decreases children's over-activity and distractibility and at the same time increases their attention and ability to concentrate.

But it does not cure the problem and often results in such negative side-effects as the suppression in normal growth of height and weight.

- Behavioural management programmes, featuring positive reinforcement and structuring learning materials and tasks in such a way that minimises errors and maximises immediate feedback and success, have been found quite useful.

- Successful modification of ADHD is claimed with cognitive behavioural training programme in which rewards for desired behaviours are combined with training in the use of verbal self-instructions (stop, think and then do). With this procedure, the ADHD children can learn to shift their attention less frequently and to behave reflectively a learning that is relatively stable over time.

Perceptual Processes

The process by which we recognise, interpret or give meaning to the information provided by sense organs is called perception. It is not just an interpretation of objects or events of the external or internal world as they exist, instead it is also a construction of those objects and events from one's own point of view. The process of meaning-making involves certain sub-processes.

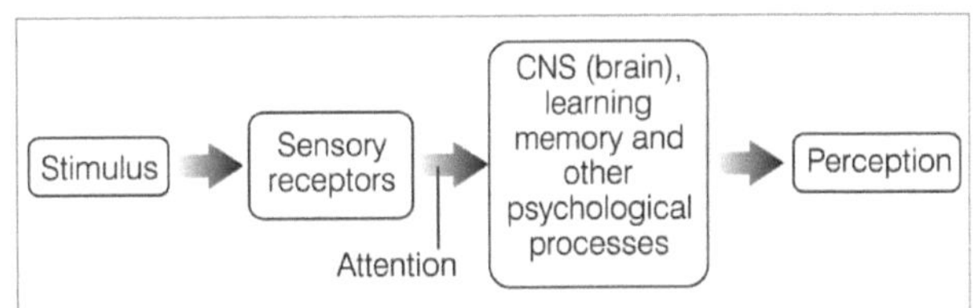

Sub-processes of Perception

Processing Approaches in Perception

There are two types of processing approaches in perception namely Bottom-up processing and Top-down processing. These are discussed as follows

1. **Bottom-up Processing** The idea that recognition process starts from the parts, and form as the basis for the recognition of the whole is known as Bottom-up Processing. The bottom-up approach lays importance on the features of stimuli in perception and considers perception as a process of mental construction.

2. **Top-down Processing** The notion that recognition process begins from the whole and leads to identification of its various parts is known as Top-down Processing.

   The top-down approach lays importance on the perceiver and considers perception as a process of recognition or identification of stimuli. In perception both the processes interact with each other to provide us with an understanding of the world.

The Perceiver

Human beings are not just mechanical and passive recipients of stimuli from the external world. They are creative beings, and try to understand the external world in their own ways. In this process their motivations and expectations, cultural knowledge, past experiences, and memories as well as values, beliefs and attitudes play an important role in giving meaning to the external world. Some of these factors are given below

Motivation

The needs and desires of a perceiver strongly influence her/his perception. People want to fulfil their needs and desires through various means.

One way to do this is to perceive objects in a picture as something that will satisfy their need. For example, some experiments were conducted to examine the influence of hunger on perception. When hungry persons were shown ambiguous pictures, they were found to perceive them as pictures of food objects more often than satiated (non-hungry) persons.

Expectations or Perceptual Sets

The expectations about what we might perceive in a given situation also influence our perception. This phenomenon of perceptual familiarisation or perceptual generalisation reflects a strong tendency to see what we expect to see even when the results do not accurately reflect external reality.

For example, if a milkman delivers milk daily at about 5:30 A.M to a person, any knocking at the door around that time is likely to be perceived by that person as the presence of the milkman even if it is someone else.

Cognitive Styles

It refers to a consistent way of dealing with our environment. It significantly affects the way we perceive the environment. There are other cognitive styles that people use in perceiving their environment. Field dependent and field independent cognitive style is the most used one in the studies.

Field dependent people perceive the external world in its totality i.e. in a global or holistic manner. On the other hand, field independent people perceive the external world by breaking it into smaller units i.e. in an analytic or differentiated manner.

Cultural Background and Experiences

Different experiences and learning opportunities available to people in different cultural settings also influence their perception. People coming from a pictureless environment fail to recognise objects in pictures.

Hudson studied the perception of pictures by African subjects noted many difficulties. Many of them were unable to identify objects shown in pictures (e.g. antelope, spear). They also failed to perceive distance in pictures and interpreted pictures incorrectly. Eskimos have been found to make fine distinction among a variety of snow that we may be unable to notice.

Some tribal groups of Siberian region have been found to differentiate among dozens of skin colours of reindeers, which we would not be able to do. These studies indicate that the perceiver plays an important role in the process of perception. People process and interpret stimuli in their own ways depending on their personal, social and cultural conditions. Due to these factors our perceptions are not only finely tunes, but also modified.

Principles of Perceptual Organisation

Our visual field is a collection of different elements, such as points, lines and colours. However, we perceive these elements as organised wholes or complete objects.

A group of researchers known as **Gestalt psychologists** tried to explain how we perceive visual field into meaningful wholes. Famous among them are **Kohler**, **Kofka**, and **Wertheimer**. Gestalt means a regular figure or a form. According to Gestalt psychologists, we perceive different stimuli not as separate elements but as an organised whole that carries a definite form.

They believe that the form of an object lies in its whole, which is different from the sum of their parts. For example, a flower pot with a bunch of flowers is a whole. If the flowers are removed, the flower pot still remains a whole. It is the configuration of the flower pot that has changed. Flower pot with flowers is one configuration, without flowers it is another configuration.

Figure Ground Segregation

The Gestalt psychologists indicate that our cerebral processes are always oriented towards the perception of a **good figure** or **pragnanz**[1]. This is the reason why we perceive everything in an organised forms. The most primitive organisation takes place in the form of **Figure Ground Segregation**. It refers to the tendency of people to separate images into figure, or object, and ground, or background.

When we look at a surface, certain aspects of the surface clearly visible as separate entities, whereas other aspects do not. For example, when we see words on a page, or a painting on a wall, or birds flying in the sky, the words, the painting, and the birds stand out from the background and are perceived as figures. Whereas the page, wall, and sky stay behind the figure and are perceived as background.

---

1 Pragnanz It is a law, which sometimes referred to as the law of good figure or the law of simplicity.

To test this experience, look at the given figure. You will see either the white part of the figure, which looks like a vase (flower pot) or the black part of the figure which looks like two faces.

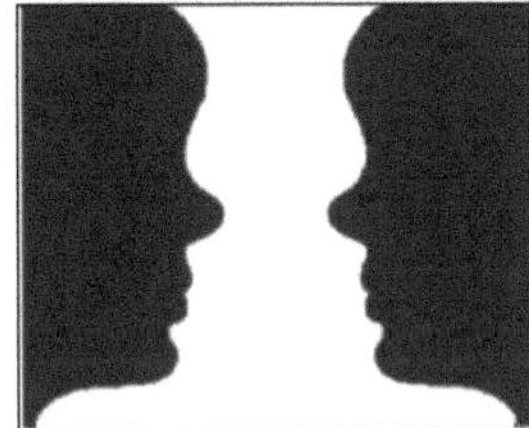
Rubin's Vase

Figure can be differentiated from the ground on the basis of the following characteristics are as follows

- Figure has a definite form while the background is relatively formless.
- Figure is more organised as compared to its background.
- Figure has a clear outline while the background has none.
- Figure stands out from the background while the background stays behind the figure.
- Figure appears more clear, limited and relatively nearer while the background appears relatively unclear, unlimited and away from us.

The Gestalt psychologists have given us several laws to explain how and why different stimuli in our visual field are organised into meaningful whole objects. These are as follows

The Principle of Proximity

According to this principle, Objects that are close together in space or time are perceived as **belonging together** or as a **group**. For example, in the figure below, the pattern of dots do not look like a square, but as a series of columns of dots and also group of dots together in rows.

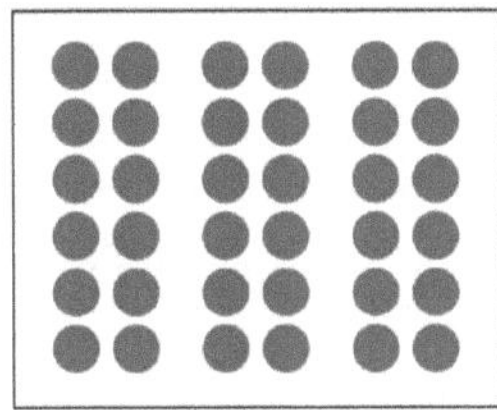
Proximity

The Principle of Similarity

According to this principle, objects that are similar to one another and have similar characteristics are **perceived as a group**. In the figure below little circles and squares are evenly spaced both horizontally and vertically so that the proximity does not come into play. Instead, we tend to see alternating columns of circles and squares.

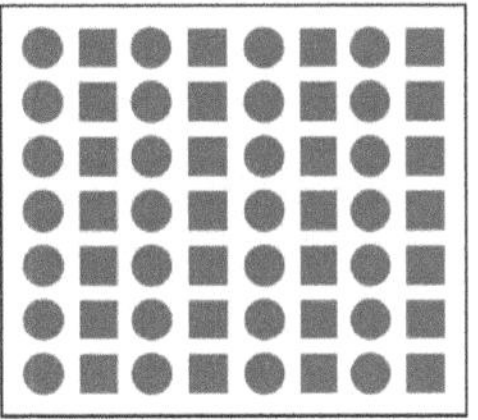
Similarity

The Principle of Continuity

This principle states that we tend to perceive objects as belonging together if they appear to form a **continuous pattern**. For instance, we are more likely to identify two lines a-b and c-d crossing than to identify four lines meeting at the center p.

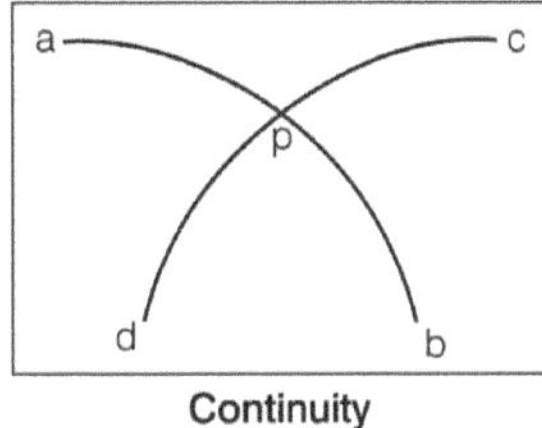
Continuity

The Principle of Smallness

According to this principle, smaller areas tend to be seen as figures against a **larger background**. In the figure below, we are most likely to see a black cross rather than a white cross within the circle because of this principle.

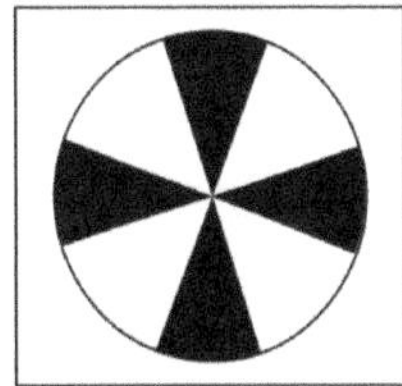
Smallness

The Principle of Symmetry

This principle suggests that symmetrical areas tend to be seen as figures against asymmetrical backgrounds. For example, in the given figure the black areas are seen as figures because they have symmetrical properties against their white asymmetrical background.

Symmetry

The Principle of Surroundedness

As per this principle, the areas surrounded by others tend to be perceived as figures. For example, the image below looks like five figures against the white background rather than word LIFT.

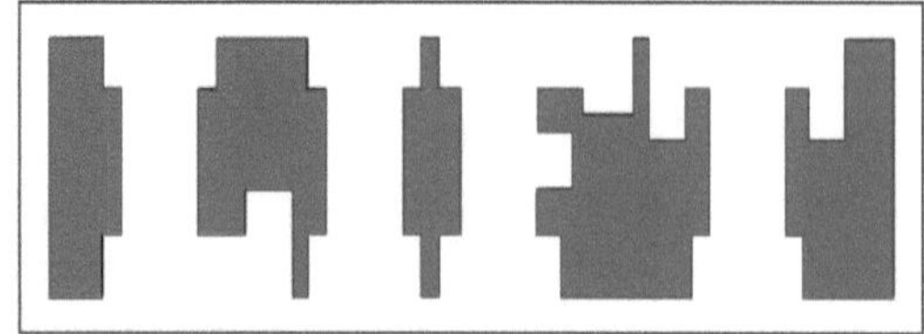

Surroundedness

The Principle of Closure

As per this principle, we try to fill the gaps in stimulation and perceive the objects as whole rather than their separate parts. In the figure below, we look at it as triangle instead of three different angles because of our tendency to fill the gaps in the object provided by our sensory output.

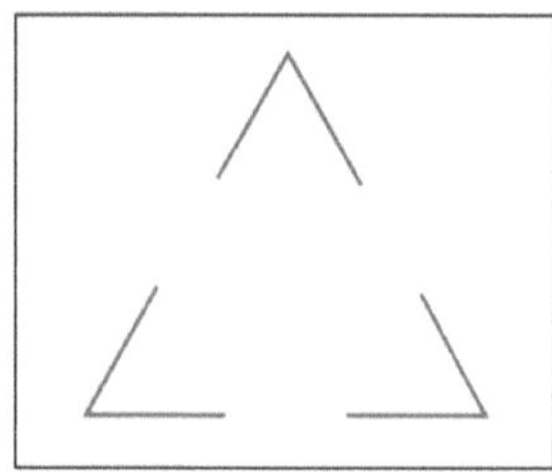

Closure

Perception of Space, Depth and Distance

The visual field or surface in which things exist, move or can be placed is called **space**. The space in which we live is organised in three dimensions. We perceive not only the spatial attributes like size, shape direction of different objects, but also the distance between the objects found in this space.

While the images of objects projected on to our retina are flat and two dimensional (left, right, up, down), we still perceive three dimensions in the space. It occurs because of our ability to transfer a two dimensional retinal vision into a three dimensional perception.

It is important in our daily life. The process of viewing the world in three dimensions is called **distance** or **Depth Perception**. In perceiving depth, we depend on two main sources of information, called **cues**.

One is called binocular cues because they require both eyes. Another is called monocular cues, because they allow us to perceive depth with just one eye. A number of such cues are used to change a two dimensional image into a three dimensional perception.

Monocular Cues

Monocular cues of depth perception are effective when the objects are viewed with only one eye. These cues are often used by artists to induce depth in two dimensional paintings. Hence, they are also known as **pictorial cues**. Some important monocular cues that help us in judging the distance and depth in two dimensional surface area

(i) **Relative Size** The size of retinal image allows us to judge distance based on our past and present experience with similar objects. As the objects get away, the retinal image becomes smaller and smaller. We tend to perceive an object farther away when it appears small and closer when it appears bigger.

(ii) **Interposition or Overlapping** These cues occur when some portion of the object is covered by another object. The overlapped object is considered farther away, whereas the object that covers it appears nearer.

(iii) **Linear Perspective** This reflects a phenomenon by which far objects appear to be closer together than the nearer objects. For example, parallel lines, such as rail tracks appear to converge with increasing distance with a vanishing point at the horizon. The more the lines converge, the farther away they appear.

(iv) **Aerial Perspective** The air contains microscopic particles of dust and moisture that make far objects look hazy or blurry. This effect is called aerial perspective. For example, distant mountains appear blue due to the scattering of blue light in the atmosphere, whereas the same mountains are perceived to be closer when the atmosphere is clear.

(v) **Light and Shade** In the light some parts of the object get highlighted, whereas some parts become darker. Highlights and shadows provide us with information about an object's distance.

(vi) **Relative Height** In relative height, larger objects are perceived as being closer to the viewer and smaller objects as being farther away. When we expect two objects to be the same size and they are not, the larger of the two will appear closer and the smaller will appear farther away.

(vii) **Texture Gradient** It represents a phenomenon by which the visual field having more density of elements is seen farther away.

(viii) **Motion Parallax** It is a kinetic monocular cue. It occurs when objects at different distances move at a different relative speed. The distant objects appear to move slowly than the objects that are close. The rate of an object's movement provides a cue to its distance. For example, when we travel in a bus, closer objects move 'against' the direction of the bus, whereas, the farther objects move 'with' the direction of the bus.

Binocular Cues

Some important cues to depth perception in three dimensional space are provided by both the eyes. Three of them have particularly been found to be interesting. These are as follows

(i) **Retinal or Binocular Disparity** Retinal disparity occurs because the two eyes have different locations in our head. They are separated from each other horizontally by a distance of about 6.5 centimeters. Because of this distance, the image formed on the retina of each eye of the same object is slightly different. This difference between the two images is called retinal disparity.

The brain interprets a large retinal disparity to mean a close object and a small retinal disparity to mean a distant object. The disparity is less for distant objects and more for the near objects.

(ii) **Convergence** When we see a nearby object, our eyes converge inward in order to bring the image on the fovea of each eye. A group of muscles send message to brain regarding the degree to which eyes are turning inward and these messages are interpreted as cues to the perception of depth. The degree of convergence decreases as the object moves further away from the observer.

For example, you can experience convergence by holding a finger in front of your nose and slowly bringing it closer. The more your eyes turn inward or converge, the nearer the object appears in space.

(iii) **Accommodation** It refers to a process by which we focus the image on the retina with the help of ciliary muscle. These muscles change the thickness of the lens of the eye. If the object gets away more than 2 meters, the muscle is relaxed. As the object moves nearer, the muscle contracts and the thickness of the lens increases. The signal about the degree of contraction of the muscle is sent to the brain, which provides the cue for distance.

Perceptual Constancies

Perception of the objects as relatively stable in spite of changes in the stimulation of the sensory receptors is called **Perceptual Constancy**. There are three types of perceptual constancies

(i) **Size Constancy** The size of an image on our retina changes with the change in the distance of the object from the eye. The further away it is, the smaller is the image. On the other hand, our experience shows that within limits, the object appears to be about the same size irrespective of its distance.

For example, when you approach your friend from a distance, your perception of the friend's size does not change much despite the fact that the retinal image (image on retina) becomes larger. The tendency for the perceived size of objects to remain relatively unchanged with changes in their distance from the observer and the size of the retinal image is called size constancy.

(ii) **Shape Constancy** In our perceptions, the shapes of familiar objects remain unchanged despite changes in the pattern of retinal image resulting from differences in their orientation. It is also called form constancy. For example, a dinner plate looks the same shape whether the image that it casts on the retina is a circle, or an ellipse, or roughly a short line (if the plate is viewed from the edge).

(iii) **Brightness Constancy** Visual objects appear constant in their degree of whiteness, greyness or blackness even though the amount of physical energy reflected from them changes considerably. In simple words, our experience of brightness does not change in spite of the changes in the amount of reflected light reaching our eyes. The tendency to maintain apparent brightness constant under different amount of illumination is called brightness constancy. For example, surface of a paper which appears white in the sunlight, is still perceived as white in the room light. Similarly, coal that looks black in the sun also looks black in room light.

Illusions

The misperceptions resulting from misinterpretation of information received by our sensory organs are generally known as illusions. They result from an external stimulus situation and generate the same kind of experience in each individual. That is why illusions are also called **primitive organisations**. Psychologists have studied illusions more commonly in the visual than in other sense modalities.

Universal and Personal Illusions

Some perceptual illusions are universal and found in all individuals. These illusions are called universal illusions or permanent illusions as they do not change with experience or practice. Some other illusions seem to differ from individual to individual; these are called personal illusions.

Geometrical Illusions

In the image we all perceive line A as shorter than line B, although both the lines are equal. This illusion is experienced even by children. There are some studies that suggest that even animals experience this illusion more or less like us.

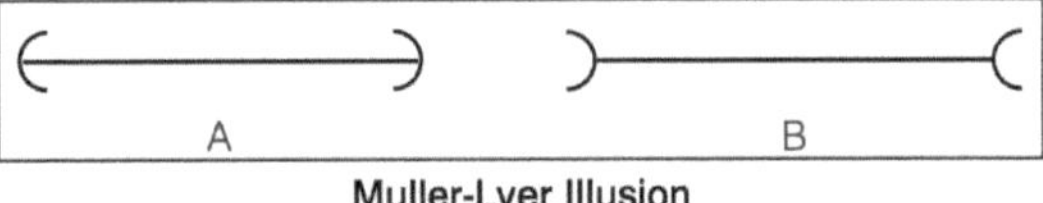

Muller-Lyer Illusion

Besides Muller-Lyer illusion, several other visual illusions are experienced by human beings, birds and animals. In the image below, we can see the illusion of vertical and horizontal lines. Although both the lines are equal, we perceive the vertical line as longer than the horizontal line.

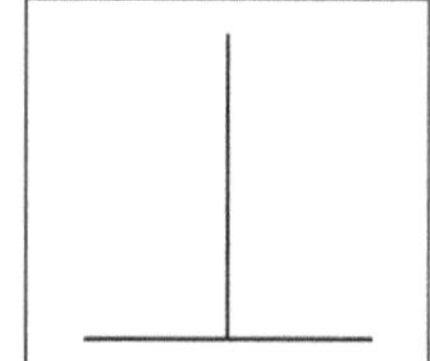

Vertical-Horizontal Illusion

Apparent Movement Illusion

This illusion is experienced when some motionless pictures are projected one after another at an appropriate rate. This illusion is referred to as **Phi-Phenomenon**. When we see moving pictures in a cinema show, we are influenced by this kind of illusion. The succession of flickering electrical lights also generate this illusion. This phenomenon can be experimentally studied with the help of an instrument by presenting two or more lights in a succession.

For the experience of this illusion, **Wertheimer** had reported the presence of appropriate level of brightness, size, spatial gap and temporal contiguity (two stimuli are experienced close together in time) of different lights to be important. In the absence of these, the light points will not appear as moving.

They will appear either as one point, or as different points appearing one after another, without any experience of motion. Experience of illusions indicates that people do not always perceive the world as it is; instead they engage its construction, sometimes based on the features of stimuli and sometimes based on their experiences in a given environment.

Socio-Cultural Influences on Perception

Several psychologists have studied the processes of perception in different socio-cultural settings. Psychologists believe that ways of people in perceiving the world must be different in some respects.

Studies Using Illusion Figures

Psychologists have used illusion figures with several groups of people living in Europe, Africa and many other places. **Segall**, **Campbell** and **Herskovits** carried out the most extensive study of illusion influence by comparing samples from remote African villages and Western urban settings.

It was found that African subjects showed greater susceptibility to horizontal-vertical illusion, whereas Western subjects showed greater susceptibility to Muller-Lyer illusion. Similar findings have been reported in other studies also. Living in dense forests the African subjects regularly experienced verticality like long trees and developed tendency to overestimate it.

The Westerners, who lived in environment characterised by right angles, developed a tendency to underestimate the length of lines characterised by enclosure, such as arrowhead. This conclusion has been confirmed in several studies. It shows that the habits of perception are learnt differently in different cultural settings.

Studies Using Pictures of Objects

In some studies people living in different cultural settings have been given pictures for identification of objects and interpretation of depth or other events represented in them.

Hudson did a seminal study in Africa and found that people who had never seen pictures, had great difficulty in recognising objects depicted in them and in interpreting depth cues like superimposition. It was indicated that informal instruction in home and habitual exposure to pictures were necessary to sustain the skill of pictorial depth perception.

Sinha and Mishra have carried out several studies on pictorial perception using a variety of pictures with people from diverse cultural settings, such as hunters and gatherers living in forests, agriculturists living in villages and people employed and living in cities. Their studies indicate that interpretation of pictures is strongly related to cultural experiences of people. While people in general can recognise familiar objects in pictures, those less exposed to pictures have difficulty in the interpretation of actions or events depicted in them.

Chapter Practice

Objective Questions

• Multiple Choice Questions

1. The relationship between stimuli and the sensations they evoke has been studied in a discipline, called_______ .
 (a) Psychology
 (b) Psychophysics
 (c) Physics
 (d) Physical science

Ans. (b) The relationship between stimuli and the sensations they evoke has been studied in a discipline, called Psychophysics.

2. The minimum value of a stimulus required to activate a given sensory system is called_______.
 (a) Minimal threshold
 (b) Absolute threshold
 (c) Difference threshold
 (d) Sensory threshold

Ans. (b) The minimum value of a stimulus required to activate a given sensory system is called Absolute threshold.

3. _______ attention is concerned mainly with the selection of a limited number of stimuli or objects from a large number of stimuli.
 (a) Divided
 (b) Selective
 (c) Sustained
 (d) Fixed

Ans. (b) Selective attention is concerned mainly with the selection of a limited number of stimuli or objects from a large number of stimuli.

4. According to which of the following theories, at once many stimuli enter our receptors creating a kind of "bottleneck" situation?
 (a) Multimode theory
 (b) Filter theory
 (c) Top Down processing
 (d) Bottom-up processing

Ans. (b) According to Filter theory, our receptors receive surplus information at a given moment, however, there is a filter which selects the stimulus which is important for higher level processing.

5. Which among the following is not a Gestalt psychologist?
 (a) Köhler
 (b) Wertheimer
 (c) Broadbent
 (d) Koffka

Ans. (c) Broadbent is not a Gestalt psychologist. He gave the filter theory of selective attention in 1956. His theory concluded that in one moment we become aware of only one stimulus, which gets access through the selective filter.

6. Consider the following statements about the multimode theory and choose the correct option.
 (i) It was developed by Johnston and Heinz (1978).
 (ii) It was developed by Broadbent (1956).
 (iii) It proposes that the stimuli not getting access to the selective filter at a given moment of time.
 (iv) It believes that attention is a flexible system that allows selection of a stimulus over others at three stages.

Options
 (a) i & iii
 (b) i & iv
 (c) ii & iii
 (d) ii & iv

Ans. (b) Multimode theory was developed by Johnston and Heinz in 1978. This theory believes that the attention is a flexible system that allows selection of a stimulus over others at three stages.

7. Shubham is able to concentrate on one topic while preparing for an exam, for a long duration. His ability to do so is known as _______ attention, which refers to our ability to maintain attention on an object or event for an extended period of time.
 (a) divided
 (b) sustained
 (c) selective
 (d) focused

Ans. (b) Shubham ability to concentrate on one object/stimulus for a prolonged period of time without being fail is known as Sustained attention.

8. Which of the following statements are true about the Attention Deficit Hyperactivity Disorder (ADHD)?
 (i) It is characterised by hostility, withdrawal, and causing harm to other people.
 (ii) It is commonly found among children of the primary school age.
 (iii) It is a behavioural problem which involves impulsivity, excessive motor activity, and an inability to pay attention to one thing at a time.

(iv) Studies have proved that certain biological factors alone are responsible for causing ADHD.

Choose the correct option

(a) i & ii   (b) i & iv

(c) ii & iii   (d) ii & iv

Ans. (c) Attention Deficit Hyperactivity Disorder is a very common behavioural disorder found among children of the primary school age. Impulsivity, hyperactivity, and an inability to pay attention to one thing at a time are some symptoms of ADHD.

9. Ankit, an 8-year-old boy, was diagnosed with ______. The psychiatrist who has taken up his case, prescribed him Ritalin. This medicine decreases children's over-activity and distractibility and at the same time increases their attention and ability to concentrate.

(a) Behavioural problems   (b) Anxiety

(c) Anger issues   (d) ADHD

Ans. (d) Ankit was diagnosed with ADHD. There is no cure or one treatment for Attention Deficit Hyperactivity Disorder. However, psychiatrists prescribe Ritalin, a drug which treats certain symptoms of ADHD.

10. The process by which we recognise, interpret or give meaning to the information provided by sense organs is called ________.

(a) attention   (b) sensation   (c) perception (d) cognition

Ans. (c) The process by which we recognise, interpret or give meaning to the information provided by sense organs is called perception .

11. According to ________ psychologists, we perceive different stimuli not as discrete elements, but as an organised "whole" that carries a definite form.

(a) Cognitive   (b) Social

(c) Behavioural   (d) Gestalt

Ans. (d) According to Gestalt psychologists, we perceive different stimuli not as discrete elements, but as an organised "whole" that carries a definite form.

12. ________ are cues for depth perception that come from the image obtained with one eye only.

(a) Binocular   (b) Illusions

(c) Monocular   (d) Pregnant

Ans. (c) Monocular are cues for depth perception that come from the image obtained with one eye only.

13. Which of the following are not binocular cues?

(i) Linear Perspective   (ii) Convergence

(iii) Motion Parallax   (iv) Accommodation

Choose the correct option

(a) i & ii   (b) ii & iv   (c) i & iii   (d) ii & iii

Ans. (c) Linear Perspective and Motion Parallax are not binocular cues. These are monocular cues whereas, convergence and accommodation are binocular cues because they require both eyes.

14. Mahima was shown some motionless pictures that were projected one after another at an appropriate rate. This illusion is referred to as (the)______.

(a) Muller-Lyer illusion   (b) Phi-phenomenon

(c) Geometrical illusions   (d) Perceptual illusions

Ans. (b) This illusion is referred to as "phi-phenomenon." This illusion is experienced when some motionless pictures are projected one after another at an appropriate rate.

• Assertion-Reasoning MCQs

Directions (Q. Nos. 1-4) *Each of these questions contains two statements, Assertion (A) and Reason (R). Each of these questions also has four alternative choices, any one of which is the correct answer. You have to select one of the codes (a), (b), (c) and (d) given below.*

(a) Both A and R are true and R is the correct explanation of A

(b) Both A and R are true but R is not the correct explanation of A

(c) Both A and R are false

(d) A is false and R is true

1. Assertion (A) Stimuli which are considered interesting or pleasing to the person will be more readily attended to.

Reason (R) Cognitive factors influence an individual's desire and readiness to focus on a particular stimulus based on certain features of the stimulus.

Ans. (a) If a stimulus is considered interesting by the person, he or she will more easily attend to it. Cognitive factors are those internal factors which include interest, attitude and preparatory set. Thus, Both A and R are true and R is the correct explanation of A.

2. Assertion (A) Sometimes we can also attend to two different things at the same time.

Reason (R) It is because of divided attention which suggests that sometimes we can be focused on more than one task in a given moment.

Ans. (a) Sometimes we can also attend to two different things at the same time as divided attention allows people to attend to two things simultaneously. This is how sometimes people talk on the phone when they are driving a car. Thus, both A and R are true and R is the correct explanation of A.

3. Assertion (A) Many stimuli simultaneously enter our receptors creating a kind of "bottleneck" situation.

Reason (R) Because according to Multimode theory attention is a flexible system that allows selection of a stimulus over others at three stages.

Ans. (b) The filter theory was given by Broadbent who suggested that an individual becomes aware of a stimulus only when it passes the selective filters. However, it was Johnston and Heinz who suggested that selection of stimulus happens in three stages. Therefore, reasoning does not justify the assertion. Thus, both A and R are true but R is not the correct explanation of A.

4. Assertion (A) The rail tracks appear to be converging to all of us.

Reason (R) Some perceptual illusions are universal and found in all individuals.

Ans. (a) The rail tracks appear to be converging to all of us because there are some illusions which are perceived and interpreted in the same way everywhere in the world. These are called permanent or universal illusions. Thus, both A and R are true and R is the correct explanation of A.

• Case Based MCQs

1. Read the case and answer the questions that follow.

The parents of Ankur, a 7-years-old boy, take him to the family practitioner because they have become increasingly concerned about his behaviour not only in school but also at home. In the first grade, he has been bored, disruptive, fighting with classmates, and rude to his teacher. At home, he cannot sit still and meals have been very unpleasant. The boy himself wonders why he is there. The parents have 2 older daughters who say their brother is a "pain" and spoiled. There were no pregnancy or birth problems and the child is on no medications. The doctor decides more information is required before any treatment is indicated. She wants careful observations of the child both at home and in school. On observing the child for a certain period, she identified that the child does not follow instructions, has difficulty in getting along with parents, and is negatively viewed by his peers. He also had difficulties in reading or learning basic subjects in schools in spite of the fact that there is no deficit in his intelligence.

(i) Identify the disorder that the child is having.
(a) Attention Deficit Hyperactivity Disorder (ADHD)
(b) Post-Traumatic Stress Disorder (PTSD)
(c) Seasonal affective disorder
(d) Dissociative disorder

Ans. (a) Ankur is showing signs of ADHD as he is hyperactive, impulsive, restless and disruptive in the classroom.

(ii) On the basis of observation, which of the following is/are characteristics of ADHD disorder?
(a) Impulsivity   (b) Excessive motor activity
(c) An inability to attend   (d) All of these

Ans. (d) ADHD involves impulsivity, difficulty in paying attention to a task at hand, hyperactive movements and high levels of distractibility.

(iii) Identify the incorrect statement with respect to this disorder
(a) This is a very common behavioural disorder found among children of the primary school age.
(b) The disorder is more prevalent among girls than among boys.
(c) There is no concrete evidence for a biological basis of the disorder.
(d) Social-psychological factors (e.g., home environment, family pathology) have been found to account for this disorder.

Ans. (b) Various research studies have shown that ADHD is more prevalent among boys than among girls. So (b) is the incorrect statement with respect to disorder.

(iv) Which of the following methods can be used to treat this disorder?
(a) Use of drug called Ritalin
(b) Behavioural management programs
(c) Cognitive behavioural training
(d) All of the above

Ans. (d) Treatment for ADHD involves medication such as Ritalin, behavioural modification methods using reinforcements, and cognitive behavioural training.

(v) ______ factors (e.g., home environment, family pathology) have been found to account for ADHD more reliably than other factors.
(a) Cognitive   (b) Social-psychological
(c) Emotional   (d) Biological

Ans. (b) Social-psychological factors (e.g., home environment, family pathology) have been found to account for ADHD more reliably than other factors.

(vi) Two statements are given in the question below as Assertion (A) and Reason (R). Select the correct option

Assertion (A) Ankur is hyperactive, impulsive, and disrupts the class with his behaviour.

Reason (R) This is because he has Attention Deficit Hyperactivity Disorder.

Codes
(a) Both A and R are true and R is the correct explanation of A
(b) Both A and R are true, but R is not the correct explanation of A
(c) A is true, but R is false
(d) A is false, but R is true

Ans. (a) ADHD is a behavioural disorder diagnosed most commonly in primary school children. It involves signs such as hyperactivity, impulsivity, distractibility, inability to pay attention to a task at hand. Therefore, both A and R are correct with R is the correct explanation of A.

Subjective Questions

• Short Answer (SA) Type Questions

1. What is Difference Threshold or Limen. Explain with example.

Ans. The smallest difference in the value of the two stimuli that is necessary to tell them that they are different is called Difference Threshold or Difference Limen (DL). This can be understood by the sugar water experiment. If we want to experience sweetness different from the previous sweetness, we need to add a minimum amount of sugar granules. The number of sugar granules added to water to generate an experience of sweetness that is different from the previous sweetness on 50 per cent of the occasions will be called the difference limen of sweetness.

Thus, Difference Threshold is the minimum amount of change in a physical stimulus that is capable of producing a sensation difference on 50 per cent of the trials.

2. What is sensation and sense modalities? Also write two functional limitations of sense organs.

Ans. The initial experience of a stimulus or an object registered by a particular sense organ is called sensation. It refers to a process through which we detect and encode a variety of physical stimuli. Different sense organs deal with different purposes. Each sense organ is highly specialised for dealing with a particular kind of information. Hence, each one of them is known as a sense modality.

Functional limitations of sense organs are as follows

- Our eyes cannot see things which are very dim or very bright.
- Our ears cannot hear very faint or very loud sounds.
- Human beings can only function within a limited range of stimulation.

3. Absolute Limen is measured across several trials.It is lowers or weakest level of stimulation. Explain Absolute Limen with example.

Ans. The minimum value of a stimulus required to activate a given sensory system is called absolute threshold or Absolute Limen (AL).

For example, one or two granules of sugar will not bring sweetness in a glass of water, but there will be some minimum amount of sugar with which a glass of water becomes sweet. This minimum quantity will be the AL of sweetness.

Here, AL is not a fixed point it differs for different individuals and situations depending on the people's organic conditions and their motivational states.

4. Explain Filter-attenuation theory of selective attention.

Ans. Filter-attenuation theory was developed by Triesman in 1962 by modifying Broadbent's theory. As per this theory, stimuli not getting access to the selective filter at a given moment of time are not completely blocked. The filter only attenuates (weakens) their strength. Thus, some stimuli manage to escape through the selective filter to reach higher levels of processing.

It is indicated that personally relevant stimuli like one's name in a collective dinner can be noticed even at a very low level of sound. Such stimuli, even though fairly weak, may also generate response occasionally by slipping through the selective filter.

5. Explain the multimode theory of selective attention?

Ans. Multimode theory of selective attention was developed by Johnston and Heinz in 1978. This theory believes that attention is a flexible system that allows selection of a stimulus over others at three stages.

These stages are as follows

- At the **first stage**, the sensory representations i.e. visual images of stimuli are constructed.
- At the **second stage**, the semantic i.e. meanings of words representations like names of objects are constructed.
- At the **third stage**, the sensory and semantic representations enter the consciousness.

6. Enumerate the factors affecting sustained attentions.

Ans. Several factors which can facilitate or interfere an individual's performance on tasks of sustained attention are as follows

(i) **Sensory Modality** Performance is found to be superior when the stimuli are auditory than when they are visual.

(ii) **Clarity of Stimuli** Intense and long lasting stimuli facilitate sustained attention and result in better performance.

(iii) **Temporal Uncertainty** When stimuli appear at regular intervals of time they are attended better than when they appear at irregular intervals.

(iv) **Spatial Uncertainty** Stimuli that appear at a fixed place are readily attended, whereas those that appear at random locations are difficult to attend.

7. During a parent-teacher meeting with a psychologist, s/he explains about Attention Deficit Hyperactivity Disorder (ADHD) to parents in order to diagnose the symptoms and provide timely proper treatment to the affected children. Discuss about ADHD.

Ans. ADHD is a very common behavioural disorder found among children of the primary school age. It is characterised by impulsivity, excessive motor activity and an inability to attend. The disorder is more common among boys than girls. If not managed properly, the attention difficulties may continue into adolescence or adult years.

Difficulty in maintaining attention is the main feature of this disorder, which gets reflected in several other domains of the child. For example, such children are highly distractible, they do not follow instructions, have difficulty in getting along with parents and are negatively viewed by their peers.

They do poorly in school, and show difficulties in reading or learning basic subjects in schools in spite of the fact that there is no deficit in their intelligence.

8. Differentiate between top-down and bottom-up approaches.

Ans. The difference between bottom-up processing and top-down processing is explained in the table are as follows

Bottom-up Processing	Top-down Processing
The idea that recognition process begins from the parts, which serve as the basis for the recognition of the whole is known as bottom-up processing.	The notion that recognition process begins from the whole, which leads to identification of its various components is known as top-down processing.
The bottom-up approach lays emphasis on the features of stimuli in perception, and considers perception as a process of mental construction.	The top-down approach lays emphasis on the perceiver, and considers perception as a process of recognition or identification of stimuli.
Example of bottom-up approach is, if you see an image of a butterfly on your screen, your eyes transmit the information to your brain, and your brain puts all of these information together.	Example of top-down processing is when while learning a new language, knowledge about letter and word meaning, syntax and other rules of language helps/aids recognition of new information.

9. Identify figure perception based on Gestalt psychologists. How do we distinguish figure as per Gestalt psychologists?

Ans. The Gestalt psychologists indicate that our cerebral processes are always oriented towards the perception of a good figure or pragnanz. The most primitive organisation takes place in the form of figure ground segregation.

Any figure can be differentiated from the ground on the basis of the following characteristics

- Figure has a definite form while the background is relatively formless.
- Figure is more organised as compared to its background.
- Figure has a clear outline while the background has none.
- Figure stands out from the background while the background stays behind the figure.
- Figure appears more clear, limited and relatively nearer while the background appears relatively unclear, unlimited and away from us.

10. What are the Binocular cues? Explain in brief

Ans. Retinal, convergence and accommodation are binocular cues.

These are described as follows

(*i*) **Retinal or Binocular Disparity** Retinal disparity occurs because the two eyes have different locations in our head. They are separated from each other horizontally by a distance of about 6.5 centimeters.

(*ii*) **Convergence** When we see a nearby object, our eyes converge inward in order to bring the image on the fovea of each eye. A group of muscles send message to brain regarding the degree to which eyes are turning inward and these messages are interpreted as cues to the perception of depth. The degree of convergence decreases as the object moves further away from the observer.

(*iii*) **Accommodation** It refers to a process by which we focus the image on the retina with the help of ciliary muscle. These muscles change the thickness of the lens of the eye.

• Long Answer (LA) Type Questions

1. Define attention. Explain its properties.   (NCERT)

Ans. The process through which certain stimuli are selected from a group of others is generally referred to as attention.

Properties of Attention Attention refers to several properties like selection, alertness, concentration and search. These are discussed in detail as follows

(i) **Selection** A large number of stimuli impinge upon our sense organs simultaneously, but we do not notice all of them at the same time. Only a selected few of them are noticed.

(ii) **Alertness** Alertness refers to an individual's readiness to deal with stimuli that appear before her/him. For example, while participating in a race in your school you might have seen the participants on the starting line in an alert state waiting for the whistle to blow in order to run.

(iii) **Concentration** Concentration refers to focusing of awareness on certain specific objects while excluding others for the moment. For example, in the classroom, a student concentrates on the teacher's lecture and ignores all sorts of noises coming from different corners of the school.

(iv) **Search** In search an observer looks for some specified subset of objects among a set of objects. For example, when you go to fetch your younger sister/brother from the school, you just look for him/her among innumerable boys and girls. All these activities require some kind of effort on the part of people. Attention in this sense refers to 'Effort Allocation'.

2. State the determinants of selective attention. How does selective attention differ from sustained attention? (NCERT)

Ans. **Selective Attention** It is concerned mainly with the selection of a limited number of stimuli or objects from a large number of stimuli. Our perceptual system has a limited capacity to receive and process information. This means that it can deal only with a few stimuli at a given moment of time.

Determinants of selective attention are generally classified as external and internal factors. These are discussed in detail as follows

(i) **External Factors** These are related to the features of stimuli. The size, intensity and motion of stimuli important determinants of attention. Large, bright and moving stimuli easily catch our attention. Stimuli, which are novel and moderately complex, also easily get into our focus. Rhythmic auditory stimuli are more readily attended than verbal narrations. Sudden and intense stimuli have a wonderful capacity to draw attention.

(ii) **Internal Factors** These lie within the individuals. These may be divided into two main categories. They are motivational factors and cognitive factors. Both are discussed in detail as follows

(a) **Motivational Factors** These are related to our biological or social needs. When we are hungry, we notice even a light smell of food. A student taking an examination is likely to focus on a teacher's instructions more than other students.

(b) **Cognitive Factors** These include factors like interest, attitude and preparatory set. Objects or events, which appear interesting are readily attended by individuals. Similarly we pay quick attention to certain objects or events to which we are favourably disposed.

Difference between Selective Attention and Sustained Attention Selective attention differs from sustained attention as selective attention is mainly concerned with the selection of limited number of stimuli from a large number of stimuli.

On the other hand sustained attention is concerned with concentration. It refers to our ability to maintain attention on an object or event for longer durations. It is also known as vigilance. Sometimes people have to concentrate on a particular task for many hours.

3. What is the main proposition of Gestalt psychologists with respect to perception of the visual field? (NCERT)

Ans. The main proposition of Gestalt psychologists with respect to perception of the visual field is that humans perceive stimuli as an organised whole which carries a definite form. The Gestalt psychologists have given us several laws to explain how and why different stimuli in our visual field are organised into meaningful whole objects. These are as follows

- **The Principle of Proximity** Objects that are close together in space or time are perceived as belonging together or as a group.
- **The Principle of Similarity** Objects that are similar to one another and have similar characteristics are perceived as a group.
- **The Principle of Continuity** This principle states that we tend to perceive objects as belonging together if they appear to form a continuous pattern.
- **The Principle of Smallness** According to this principle, smaller areas tend to be seen as figures against a larger background.
- **The Principle of Symmetry** This principle suggests that symmetrical areas tend to be seen as figures against asymmetrical backgrounds.
- **The Principle of Surroundedness** As per this principle, the areas surrounded by others tend to be perceived as figures.
- **The Principle of Closure** We try to fill the gaps in stimulation and perceive the objects as whole rather than their separate parts.

4. How can we form a stable perception of an object seen from any position and in any intensity of light? Justify.

Ans. Perception of the objects as relatively stable in spite of changes in the stimulation of the sensory receptors is called perceptual constancy. There are three types of perceptual constancies discussed as follows

(i) **Size Constancy** The size of an image on our retina changes with the change in the distance of the object from the eye. The further away it is, the smaller is the image. On the other hand, our experience shows that within limits, the object appears to be about the same size irrespective of its distance.

The tendency for the perceived size of objects to remain relatively unchanged with changes in their distance from the observer and the size of the retinal image is called size constancy.

(ii) **Shape Constancy** In our perceptions, the shapes of familiar objects remain unchanged despite changes in the pattern of retinal image resulting from differences in their orientation. It is also called form constancy.

(iii) **Brightness Constancy** Visual objects appear constant in their degree of whiteness, greyness or blackness even though the amount of physical energy reflected from them changes considerably. The tendency to maintain apparent brightness constant under different amount of illumination is called brightness constancy.

For example, surface of paper which appears white in the sunlight is still perceived as white in the room light. Similarly coal that looks black in the sun also looks black in room light.

5. How do socio-cultural factors influence our perceptions? **(NCERT)**

Ans. Several psychologists have studied the processes of perception in different socio-cultural settings. Psychologists that believe ways of people in perceiving the world must be different in some respects.

Studies using Illusion Figures Psychologists have used illusion figures with several groups of people living in Europe, Africa and many other places.

Segall, Campbell and Herskovits carried out the most extensive study of illusion influence by comparing samples from remote African villages and Western urban settings.

It was found that African subjects showed greater susceptibility to horizontal-vertical illusion, whereas Western subjects showed greater susceptibility to Muller-Lyer illusion. Living in dense forests the African subjects regularly experienced verticality like long trees and developed tendency to overestimate it.

The Westerners, who lived in environment characterised by right angles, developed a tendency to underestimate the length of lines characterised by enclosure, such as arrowhead. It shows that the habits of perception are learnt differently in different cultural settings.

Studies using Pictures of Objects In some studies people living in different cultural settings have been given pictures for identification of objects and interpretation of depth or other events represented in them. Hudson did a seminal study in Africa and found that people who had never seen pictures, had great difficulty in recognising objects depicted in them and in interpreting depth cues like superimposition. It was indicated that informal instruction in home and habitual exposure to pictures were necessary to sustain the skill of pictorial depth perception.

6. Discuss about the figure ground segregation. How figure can be differentiated from the ground?

Ans. Figure ground segregation is a type of perceptual grouping that is important for recognising objects through vision. The Gestalt psychologists indicate that our cerebral processes are always oriented towards the perception of a **good figure** or **pragnanz**. This is the reason why we perceive everything in an organised forms.

The most primitive organisation takes place in the form of **Figure Ground Segregation**. It refers to the tendency of people to separate images into figure, or object, and ground, or background.

When we look at a surface, certain aspects of the surface clearly visible as separate entities, whereas other aspects do not. For example, when we see words on a page, or a painting on a wall, or birds flying in the sky, the words, the painting, and the birds stand out from the background and are perceived as figures. Whereas the page, wall, and sky stay behind the figure and are perceived as background.

Figure can be differentiated from the ground on the basis of the following characteristics are as follows

- Figure has a definite form while the background is relatively formless.
- Figure is more organised as compared to its background.
- Figure has a clear outline while the background has none.

• Case Based Questions

1. Read the passage and answer the questions that follow.

Raj and Sanya are a couple and they were going out for dinner one night. While driving his car, Raj starts talking on the phone with a business client. This worries Sanya and then she asks him to put the phone down while he is driving as he will not be paying attention on the road. He hangs up and then they both get into an argument

Raj is of the view that if a person is capable of focusing on two tasks efficiently at a given time then they should do that. He tells her that he is confident about his driving skills and he has talked on call while driving several times before.

On the other hand, Sanya thinks paying attention to one task at a time is more important and leads to efficient performance. She believes that focusing on two things at once can lead to inefficiency. The person will not be able to give their best on either of the tasks.

(i) Identify and briefly describe the type of attention, Raj and Sanya are debating over.

Ans. Raj is engaging in divided attention as his focus is on driving as well as talking on the phone, whereas, Sanya believes selective attention is more appropriate as it requires one to pay full attention to one task at a time.

(ii) What are the factors which influence selective attention?

Ans. Several factors influence selective attention. These generally relate to the characteristics of stimuli and the characteristics of individuals. They are generally classified as "external" (related to the features of stimuli) and "internal" factors (lie within the individual).

(iii) What are motivational factors? Elucidate with an example.

Ans. Motivational factors relate to our biological or social needs. When we are hungry, we notice even a faint smell of food. A student taking an examination is likely to focus on a teacher's instructions more than other students.

2. Read the passage and answer the questions that follow.

In a classroom, a teacher decides to conduct a play activity with a group of third standard students. For this, they were given some objects such as blocks and circles to play with. Each of them was asked to place those objects as it pleases them. The teacher decides to observe how the students carry out this activity.

The first student picks the circles and puts all the circles very close to each other. She keeps them in such a way that there are no gaps in between and all the circles are in close proximity.

The second picks up blocks and circles. He put all the blocks in one row close to one another and all the circles close together in a different row. It looked as if blocks belonged to one group and circles to another.

The third picks up both circles and blocks and decides to make a continuous chain with those blocks and circles. She wanted to create a big circle with all of the blocks and circles together.

(i) Which school of psychology has laid down several perceptual principles which explain why we perceive everything in an organised form?

Ans. The Gestalt school of thought has given us several laws to explain how and why different stimuli in our visual field are organised into meaningful whole objects.

(ii) Identify the gestalt principles from the given passage.

Ans. First student's display is based on the principle of proximity, the second student's display is based on the principle of similarity and the third student's display is based on the Principle of Continuity.

(iii) What does the principle of closure and principle of surroundedness mean?

Ans. The principle of closure states that we tend to fill the gaps in stimulation and perceive the objects as whole rather than their separate parts. According to the principle of surroundedness, the areas surrounded by others tend to be perceived as figures.

3. Refer to the picture given below and answer the questions by choosing the most appropriate option.

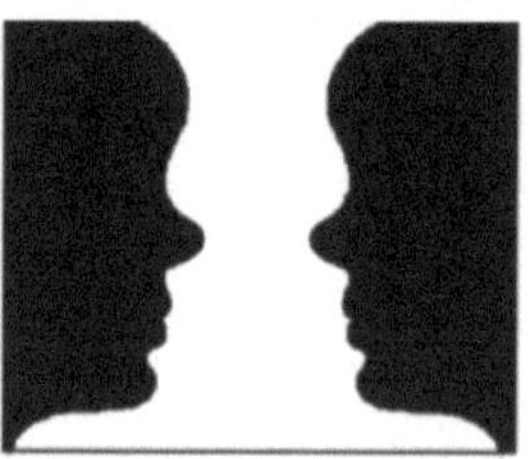

(i) What is the name of the figure given above?

Ans. Rubin's vase is a perceptual illusion wherein two images appear in the same image. One is incorporated in the black part and the other is seen in the white part of it.

(ii) Which of the following phenomena does this picture represent?

Ans. This figure represents Figure-ground segregation phenomenon. In this, we tend to see some aspects of an image as the figure while the other aspects as the background. For ex, in Rubin's vase, you may see faces as figure or the vase as figure.

(iii) What do you mean by Gestalt?

Ans. Gestalt means a regular figure or a form. As per this theory, we perceive different stimuli not as different elements, but as an organised whole that carries a definite form.

Chapter Test

Multiple Choice Questions

1. One's ability to distinguish find details is called
(a) Sensation
(b) Perception
(c) Visual acuity
(d) Apperception

2. ________ are cues for depth perception that come from the image obtained with one eye only.
(a) Binocular cues
(b) Illusions
(c) Monocular cues
(d) Pragnanz

3. Artists mostly use ________ to create an impression of depth on a flat surface.
(a) monocular cues
(b) binocular cues
(c) form perception
(d) convergence

4. The tendency to maintain apparent brightness constant under different amounts of illumination is called ______ constancy.
(a) shape
(b) size
(c) brightness
(d) colour

5. The number of objects one can attend to at a brief exposure (i.e. a fraction of a second) is called ______ .
(a) Limit of attention
(b) Span of attention
(c) Capacity of attention
(d) Sustained attention

Short Answer Type Questions

6. Define attention

7. What do you mean by 'bottom-up processing'?

8. What do you mean by cognitive styles?

9. Discuss in brief 'Attention Deficit Hyperactivity Disorder' (ADHD).

10. Explain the role of binocular cues in the perception of depth.

Long Answer Type Questions

11. Discuss monocular cues of perception.

12. Discuss socio-cultural influences on perception.

13. Describe the causal factors of ADHD and the treatment for ADHD.

14. Discuss perceptual constancy. Describe the three types of perceptual constancies.

Answers

1. (a)   *2.* (c)   *3.* (a)   *4.* (c)   *5.* (b)

CHAPTER 03

Learning

In this Chapter...

- Meaning and Nature of Learning
- Paradigms of Learning
- Classical Conditioning
- Operant Conditioning
- Key Learning Processes
- Other Paradigms of Learning (Observational, Cognitive, Verbal and Skill Learning)

Introduction

At the time of birth every human baby is equipped with the capacity to make a limited number of responses. These responses occur reflexively whenever appropriate stimuli are present in the environment. As the child grows and matures, she/he becomes capable of making diverse types of responses.

As one grows older, one observes many events or objects and learns their distinct features. It is all due to learning that a person becomes hard working or indolent, socially knowledgeable, skilled and professionally competent. Each individual manages her or his life and solves all kinds of problems because of the capacity to learn and adapt.

Nature of Learning

Learning is a psychological process which gradually develops in human being. Due to learning, a person becomes hard working, socially knowledgeable, skilled and professionally competent. Learning can be defined as any relatively permanent change in behaviour or behavioural potential produced by experience. It refers to a range of changes that take place as a result of one's experience. Relatively permanent changes which occur due to practice and experience are examples of learning.

Features of Learning

There are different features for the process of learning. These are discussed as follows

Learning by Experience

Learning always involves some kinds of experience. We experience an event occurring in a certain sequence during different occasions. If an event happens then it may be followed by some other events. For example, students learn that if the bell rings in the hostel in the evening, then it implies that the dinner is ready to be served. If some action is repeatedly done in a specified manner and it gives satisfaction, this experience leads to the formation of habit.

Sometimes a single experience can lead to learning. For example, if a child strike a matchstick on the side of match box and his finger is burnt, he becomes more careful while handling the matchbox in future.

Temporary Behavioural Changes

In the process of learning, behavioural changes that occur due to learning are relatively permanent. It should be distinguished from the behavioural changes that are neither permanent nor learned.

Sometimes behavioural changes also happen due to continuous exposure to stimuli. It is called **habituation** which is not due to learning. For example, the sound of loudspeaker distracts us from whatever we are doing. Gradually, we make some **orienting reflexes**[1] and become habituated with this sound. For example, changes in behaviour sometimes occur due to the effects of fatigue, habituation and drugs.

Learning Involves Sequence of Psychological Events

Psychologists suggest that learning process always involves the following sequences

(*i*) Do a pre-test to know how much the person knows before learning.

(*ii*) Present the list of words to be remembered for a fixed time.

(*iii*) During this time the list of words is processed towards acquiring new knowledge.

(*iv*) After processing is complete, new knowledge is acquired, thus learning is completed.

(*v*) After sometime, the processed information is recalled by the person.

Learning is an Inferred Process but Different from Performance

When a student recites a poem, he gives his performance. By seeing his performance, the teacher infers that the student has now learned the poem which is not done by him previously. By comparing the number of words which a person now knows as compared to what she/he knew, the teacher can infer that learning took place.

Thus, learning is an inferred process and is different from performance. Performance is a person's observed behaviour or response or action.

Paradigms of Learning

In psychology, we have seen that learning takes place in many ways. There are different types of methods, some are used in acquisition of simple responses while other methods are used in the acquisition of complex responses. **Conditioning**[2] is the simplest kind of learning. Two types of conditioning have been identified. The first one is **classical conditioning** and the second is **instrumental/operant conditioning**.

Besides these, there are observational learning, cognitive learning, verbal learning, concept learning and skill learning.

Classical Conditioning

Classical conditioning is a procedure in which a biological stimulus (e.g. food) is paired with a previously neutral stimulus e.g. bell. It is a type of learning that happens unconsciously. It is also known as **respondent conditioning**. **Ivan P Pavlov** was the first one to experiment this type of learning.

Experiment of Pavlov

Pavlov designed an experiment using dog to understand this process. He observed that dogs secreted saliva whenever they saw the plate in which they were served food. We all know that saliva secretion is a reflexive response to food or something in the mouth.

In the first part of the experiment, a dog was kept in the box to conduct experiment. A simple surgery was conducted, and one end of a tube was inserted in the dog's jaw and the other end of tube was put in a measuring glass. This was used to measure the amount of saliva dog secreted.

In the second part of the experiment, the dog was kept hungry and placed in harness with one end of the tube ending in the jaw and the other end in the glass jar. A bell was rang and immediately after the sound, food(meat powder) was served to dog.

The dog was allowed to eat it. This routine was continued for next few days i.e immediately after ringing the bell, food was given to the dog. After a number of such trials, a test trial was conducted in which, everything was repeated except that food was not served to dog after ringing the bell.

The dog still secreted saliva after listening to the sound of the bell, expecting its food to be served, because dog thought bell and food were connected.

This connection between bell and food resulted in obtaining a new response by the dog, i.e secreting saliva to the sound of bell. This has been called conditioning.

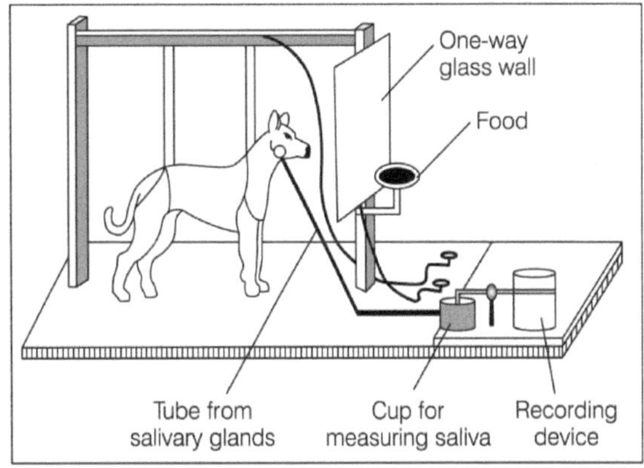

A Dog in Pavlovian Harness for Conditioning

---

1 **Orienting Reflexes** It is an organism's immediate response to a change in its environment.
2 Conditioning Conditioning is the process of training a person or animal to do something or to behave in a certain way in a particular situation.

Components of Conditioning in Pavlov Experiment

Usually all dogs salivate when they are served with food. Hence, food is an **Unconditioned Stimulus** (US) and secretion of saliva after that is called an **Unconditioned Response** (UR). But after conditioning, due to bell sound dog started salivation. So, here the bell becomes a **Conditioned Stimulus** (CS) and saliva secretion is called **Conditioned Response** (CR).

This kind of conditioning is called classical conditioning. The learning process in classical conditioning is one of **S-S learning** i.e one stimulus (e.g. sound of bell) becomes a signal for another stimulus (e.g food). It means one stimulus causes occurrence of another stimulus.

We experience a number of examples of classical conditioning in our daily life. For example, imagine you have just finished your lunch and you are feeling satisfied. Then you see some sweet dish served on the adjoining table. This signals its taste in your mouth, and triggers the secretion of saliva. You feel like eating it. This is a conditioned response (CR).

Another example is, in the early stages of childhood, children naturally afraid of any loud noise. Suppose a small child catches an inflated balloon which bursts in her/his hands making a loud noise.

The child becomes afraid. Now the next time she/he is made to hold a balloon, it becomes a signal or cue for noise and elicits fear response. This happens because of contiguous presentation of balloon as a conditioned stimulus (CS) and loud noise as an unconditioned stimulus (US).

Determinants of Classical Conditioning

Time relations between stimuli, types of unconditioned stimuli and intensity of conditioned stimuli are the main determinants of classical conditioning. These are explained as follows

Time Relations between Stimuli

There are basically four types of classical conditioning procedures. The first three are called **forward conditioning** procedures and the fourth one is called **backward conditioning** procedure.

These procedures can be explained in the following ways

(*i*) When the CS and US are started together, it is called **simultaneous conditioning**.

(*ii*) When CS is started first before the start of US and CS ends first before the end of US, it is called **delayed conditioning**. The delayed conditioning procedure is the most effective way of acquiring a Conditioned Response (CR).

(*iii*) When CS starts and ends before the start of US, and if there is a time gap between the two, it is called **trace conditioning**.

(*iv*) When US comes before the start of CS, it is called **backward conditioning**. The acquisition of response under backward conditioning procedure is very rare.

Type of Unconditioned Stimuli

There are two types of unconditioned stimuli used in studying classical conditioning. They are as follows

(*i*) **Appetitive** This stimuli automatically draws out approach responses like eating, drinking, caressing, etc. It means these kind of events will make us feel good and we would love to participate in such events. These kind of responses give satisfaction and pleasure. Appetitive classical conditioning is slower and it requires large number of acceptance trials.

(*ii*) **Aversive** This stimuli like noise, bitter taste, electric shock, painful injections, etc are painful, harmful and draws out avoidance and escape responses. Aversive classical conditioning is established in one, two or three trials depending on the intensity of the aversive Unconditioned Stimulus (US).

Intensity of Conditioned Stimuli

Intensity influences the direction of both appetitive and aversive classical conditioning. More intense conditioned stimuli are more effective in accelerating the acceptance of conditioned responses. It means that more intense the conditioned stimulus, the less number of acquisition trials are needed for conditioning.

Relationship of Stages of Conditioning and Operations

Stages of Conditioning	Nature of Stimulus	Nature of Response
Before	Food (US) Sound of the Bell	Salivation (UR) Alertness (No specific response)
During	Sound of the Bell (CS)+ Food (US)	Salivation (UR)
After	Sound of the Bell (CS)	Salivation (CR)

Instrumental/Operant Conditioning

Instrumental/operant conditioning is a learning process through which strength of the behaviour is modified by **reward** or **punishment**.

BF Skinner was the first one to do research about this type of conditioning. Skinner studied about operants. Operants are those behaviours or responses which are shown by animals and humans voluntarily and are under their control.

The term operant is used because the organism operates on the environment. Conditioning of operant behaviour is called operant conditioning.

Experiment by Skinner

Skinner conducted his studies on rats and pigeons in specially made boxes called **Skinner Box**. One hungry rat is placed inside the box such that it could not come out but just move inside the box as shown in the figure.

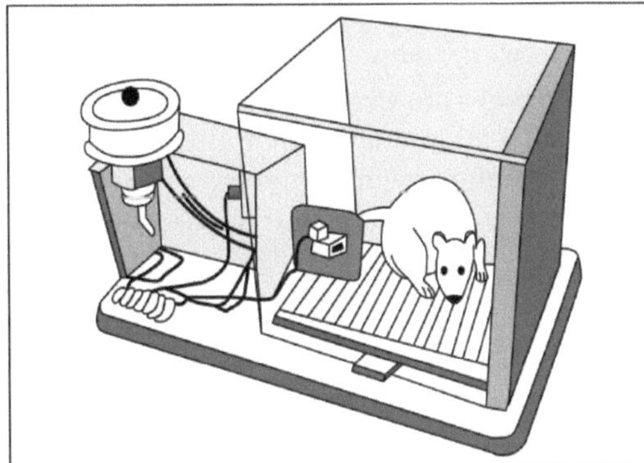

Skinner Box

A lever which was connected to a food container was kept at the top of the chamber. While moving around and pawing the walls which is called **exploratory behaviour**[3], the rat accidentally presses the lever and a food pellet drops on the plate, and the hungry rat eats it. In next trial, after a while the exploratory behaviour again starts and this continues. As number of trials increases, the time taken to press the lever by the rat for the food decreases.

Conditioning is complete when rat presses the lever immediately after it is kept in the chamber. In this scenario, lever pressing is an **operant response** and getting food is its consequence. As the response is instrumental in getting the food, this type of learning is called **instrumental conditioning**.

We experience a number of examples of instrumental conditioning in our everyday life. For example, children who want to have some sweets in the absence of their mother learn to locate the jar in which mother hides the sweets for safekeeping and eat it.

Children learn to be polite and say 'please' to get favours from their parents and others. One learns to operate mechanical gadgets such as radio, camera, T.V., etc. based on the principle of instrumental conditioning. As a matter of fact human beings learn shortcuts to attain desired goals or ends through instrumental conditioning.

Determinants of Operant Conditioning

Operant or instrumental conditioning is a form of learning in which behaviour is learned, maintained or changed based on its consequences. Such consequences are called **reinforcers**.

Reinforcers are events or stimulus which increase the probability of the occurrence of a desired response. Reinforcer has following main features which affect the direction and strength of a response. These are of following types

- Positive or negative
- Number or frequency
- Quality i.e. superior or inferior
- Schedule i.e. continuous or partial.

These features influence the process of operant conditioning. Besides these factors, there is another factor that influences this type of learning i.e. the nature of the response or behaviour that is to be conditioned. Operant learning is also influenced by the interval or length of time that lapses between occurrence of response and reinforcement.

Classical and Operant Conditioning: Differences

1. In classical conditioning, the responses are under the control of some stimulus because they are reflexes, automatically elicited by the appropriate stimuli. Such stimuli are selected as US and responses elicited by them as US. Thus Pavlovian conditioning, in which US elicits responses, is often called **respondent conditioning**.

   In operant conditioning, responses are under the control of the organism and are voluntary responses or 'operants'. Thus, in the two forms of conditioning different types of responses are conditioned.

2. In classical conditioning, the CS and US are well-defined, but in operant conditioning CS is not defined. It can be inferred but is not directly known.

3. In classical conditioning, the experimenter controls the occurrence of US, while in operant conditioning the occurrence of the reinforcer is under the control of the organism that is learning. Thus, for us in classical conditioning the organism remains passive, while in operant conditioning the subject has to be active in order to be reinforced.

4. In the two forms of conditioning, the technical terms used to characterise the experimental proceedings are different. Moreover what is called reinforcer in operant conditioning is called US in classical conditioning. A US has two functions. In the beginning it elicits the response and also reinforces the response to be associated and elicited later on by the CS.

Key Learning Processes

Different processes that are involved in learning through either classical or operant conditioning are as follows

1. Reinforcement
2. Extinction or non-occurrence of learned response
3. Generalisation and discrimination
4. Spontaneous recovery

---

3 Exploratory Behaviour This type of behaviour or actions are aimed at understanding, exploring and acquiring information about the environment.

1. Reinforcement

It is the activity of managing a reinforcer by the experimenter. Reinforcers are stimuli that increase the rate or probability of the responses that precede.

Types of Reinforcement

Reinforcement may be positive or negative. These are discussed as follows

- **Positive Reinforcement** It involves stimuli that have pleasant consequences. Positive reinforcers satisfy needs which include food, water, medals, praise, money, status, information etc. They strengthen and maintain the responses that have caused them to occur.
- **Negative Reinforcement** It involves unpleasant and painful stimuli. Responses that lead organisms to get rid of painful stimuli or avoid and escape from them provide **negative reinforcement**. So negative reinforcement leads to learning of avoidance and escape responses. For example, we learn to put on woollen clothes, burn firewood or use electric heaters to avoid the unpleasant cold weather. We learn to move away from dangerous stimuli because they provide negative reinforcement.
- Negative reinforcement is not a punishment. Use of punishment reduces or suppresses the response. But a negative reinforcer increases the probability of avoidance or escape response. For example, drivers and co-drivers wear their seat belts to avoid getting injured in case of an accident or to avoid being fined by the traffic police. No punishment suppresses a response permanently, it is no matter how strong the response is.
- It is observed that mild and delayed punishment has no effect. The stronger the punishment, the more lasting is the suppression effect but it is not permanent. Sometimes punishment has no effect irrespective of its intensity. Contrary to this, the punished person may develop dislike and hatred for the punishing agent or the person who administers the punishment.

Number of Reinforcement

Number of reinforcement refers to the number of trials on which an organism has been reinforced or rewarded. Amount of reinforcement means how much of reinforcing stimulus (food, water, intensity of pain causing agent) one receives on each trial. Quality of reinforcement refers to the kind of reinforcer.

The course of operant conditioning is usually accelerated to an extent as the number, amount and quality of reinforcement increases.

Schedules of Reinforcement

The arrangement of the delivery of reinforcement during conditioning trials are considered as the reinforcement schedule. Each schedule of reinforcement influences the course of conditioning in its own way.

So, conditioned responses occur with differential characteristics. The organism being subjected to operant conditioning may be given reinforcement in every acquisition trial or in some trials it is given and in others it is omitted. Reinforcement may be continuous or intermitten which means that

- (i) When a desired response is reinforced every time it occurs we call it continuous reinforcement.
- (ii) When responses are sometimes reinforced, sometimes not, we call it intermitten reinforcement. It is also called as **partial reinforcement**. It produces greater resistance to extinction than continuous reinforcement.

Delayed Reinforcement

- Delay in the delivery of reinforcement leads to poorer level of performance.
- Children prefer smaller rewards immediately after doing the chore rather than a big one after a long gap.

Other Types of Reinforcement

- The reinforcers may be primary or secondary.
- A primary reinforcer is biologically important since it determines the organisms survival, e.g. food for a hungry organism.
- A secondary reinforcer is one which has acquired characteristics of the reinforcer because of the organism's experience with the environment. We use money, praise and grades as reinforcers which are known as secondary reinforcers.

2. Extinction

Extinction means disappearance of a learned response due to removal of reinforcement from the situation in which the response used to occur. If the occurrence of CS-CR is not followed by the US in classical conditioning or lever pressing is no more followed by food pellets in the Skinner box. Then the learned behaviour will gradually be weakened and ultimately disappear. It is observed that learning shows resistance to extinction. In other words, even though the learned response is now not reinforced, it would continue to occur for sometime. However, with increasing number of trials without reinforcement, the response strength gradually decreases and ultimately it stops occurring. How long a learned response shows resistance to extinction depends on a number of factors.

Different scenarios affecting resistance to extinction are as follows

- (i) Resistance to extinction increases and learned response reaches its highest level and performance gets stabilised, when number of reinforced trials are increased. Hereafter, response strength is not affected by number of trials.
- (ii) Resistance to extinction increases when number of reinforcements are increased during acquisition trials. After a point, if we increase number of reinforcements, the resistance to extinction decreases.

(*iii*) Resistance to extinction increases if reinforcement is delayed during acquisition trials. Continuous reinforcement makes the learned response to be less resistant to extinction and more in case of partial reinforcement.

3. Generalisation and Discrimination

The phenomenon of responding similarly to similar stimuli is known as generalisation. For example, if a child has learned the location of a jar of a certain size and shape in which sweets are kept, the child can find the jar and obtains the food even in the absence of his mother. This is called **learned operant**.

Further mother keeps the sweet in another jar at a different location and the child can locate and obtains it. Now it is also an example of **generalisation**.

Discrimination is a response due to difference. Discriminative response depends on the discrimination capacity or discrimination learning of the organism. For example, if a child is conditioned to be afraid of a person with a long moustache and wearing black cloth, he shows signs of fear whenever he meets a person with a beard and in black clothes in future. The child's fear is generalised. He meets another stranger who is wearing grey clothes and is clean shaven. Then the child shows no fear.

4. Spontaneous Recovery

Spontaneous recovery occurs after a learned response has extinguished. For example, if an organism has learned to make a response for getting reinforcement, then the response is extinguished and some time lapses. Now we can ask a question, whether the response is completely extinguished and will not occur if the CS is presented.

It has been shown that after lapse of considerable time, the learned or conditioned response recovers and occurs to the conditioned stimulus. The amount of spontaneous recovery depends on the duration of the time lapsed after the extinction session. Recovery of the learned response is stronger if the duration of time lapse is longer and such a recovery occurs spontaneously.

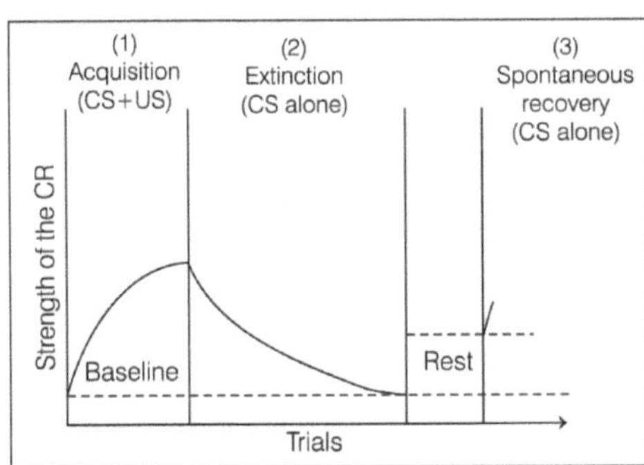

Phenomenon of Spontaneous Recovery

Learned Helplessness

Learned helplessness occurs when people or animals feel helpless to avoid negative situations. It is one of the causes for depression. **Seligman** and **Maier** conducted experiments on dogs to demonstrate this phenomenon.

They subjected to dogs to sound (CS) and electric shock (US) using classical conditioning procedure. The animal had no scope to escape or avoid the shock. This process was repeated a number of times. The dog could escape the shock by pressing their heads against the wall, but the dog did not attempt to escape. This behaviour of dog was called **learned helplessness**.

When humans encounter continuous failures in a set of tasks, then they show learned helplessness. It is measured in terms of subject's ability and persistence before they give the task. Continuous failure results in little persistence and poor performance. Number of studies also show that persistent depression is caused due to learned helplessness.

Other Paradigms of Learning

Learning takes place in many ways. There are some methods that are used in obtaining simple responses while other methods are used in obtaining complex responses.

Observational Learning

In this type, learning happens by observing others. It was earlier called **imitation**. Bandura and his colleagues studied observational learning in detail. It is also called **social learning** because humans learn social behaviour through this. Individuals try to copy the behaviour of others in many situations and this is called **modeling**.

Experimental Study by Bandura

Bandura conducted an experimental study in which he has shown a movie of five minute duration to children. The film has a large room with number of toys including a large sized Bobo doll. Now a grown-up boy enters the room. Boy shows aggressive behaviour towards toys and he hits the bobo doll, throws it on the floor, kicking it and sitting on it. This film has three versions, children were shown. These were

(*i*) That the boy (model) was rewarded for being aggressive.

(*ii*) That the boy was punished for being aggressive.

(*iii*) That the boy was neither punished nor rewarded.

Now when children were kept in a similar room with toys, children behaved differently i.e. children who saw boy being awarded behaved in most aggressive manner and children who saw boy being punished behaved in least aggressive manner.

Thus, in observational learning observers get knowledge by observing model's behaviour, but performance is influenced by model's behaviour being rewarded or punished.

Children learn most of the social behaviours by observing and emulating adults. Aggressiveness, pro-social behaviour, courtesy, politeness, diligence, laziness are acquired by this method of learning.

Cognitive Learning

Cognitive learning defines learning as a behavioural change based on the information obtained about the environment. In cognitive learning, there is a change in what the learner knows rather than what she/he does. This kind of learning can be seen in insight learning and latent learning.

Insight Learning

In insight learning, solution to a problem suddenly becomes clear. **Kohler** conducted experiments with chimpanzees to demonstrate this kind of learning. He placed chimpanzees in an enclosed play area where food was kept outside their reach. They were provided with some boxes and poles. Chimpanzees very soon learnt how to use these boxes and poles to get the food. They did not do it by trial and error method, but all of a sudden, they would stand on a box and use a pole to strike a banana.

This kind of learning is called insight learning i.e. a sudden solution to the problem. Once the solution is found, it can be repeated immediately the next time the problem appears. So, this learning is not the result of a specific set of conditioned stimuli and responses but a cognitive relationship between a means and an end (goal). Thus, insight learning can be generalised to other similar problems.

Latent Learning

Another type of cognitive learning is known as latent learning. In this learning, a new behaviour is learned but not shown until reinforcement is provided for displaying it. **Tolman** conducted experiments to show this kind of learning. He kept two groups of rats in a maze i.e. a complex network of paths and passages.

In one group, rats found food at the end of maze and next time they learned to find the way very quickly. But in second group, since they were not rewarded (no food), they did not show the signs of learning. But later when rats were rewarded, they ran through the maze as efficiently as the rewarded group. Tolman observed that rats developed a cognitive map of the maze, i.e. a representation in brain about the key locations and directions to reach their goal.

Verbal Learning

Verbal learning is limited to human beings, because they acquire knowledge about different objects, events and other things in terms of words. Psychologists developed number of methods to study this kind of learning. Each method uses some kind of verbal material like nonsense syllables, familiar words, unfamiliar words, sentences and paragraphs.

Methods Used in Studying Verbal Learning

Some methods used in studying verbal learning are as follows

1. Paired-Associates Learning

This method is used in learning some foreign language which is similar to mother tongue words. This method is similar to S-S conditioning and S-R learning. First, a list of paired associates is prepared. The first word of the pair is used as stimulus and the second word as the response.

Members of each pair may be from the same language or two different languages. The learner is first shown both the stimulus response pairs together and is instructed to remember and recall the response after the presentation of each stimulus term. After that a learning trial begins when one by one the stimulus words are presented and the participant tries to give the correct response term.

2. Serial Learning

This learning is to know how participants learn the list of words in a given order. In first part of the experiment lists of verbal items are prepared i.e. nonsense syllables, most familiar or least familiar words, interrelated words etc.

The participant is now given the list of verbal items and is supposed to tell the items in the same serial order as per the list. This procedure is called **serial anticipation method**. Learning trials continue until the participant correctly anticipates all the items in the given order.

3. Free Recall

In this method, participants are presented with a list of words and each word is shown for a fixed amount of time. Participant now has to recall all the words in any order.

Words in the list may be interrelated or unrelated. More than ten words are included in the list. The presentation order of the words varies from trial to trial. This method is used to study about how participants arrange words for storage in memory. Studies show that words at start and end are easy to remember compared to those placed in the middle.

Determinants of Verbal Learning

There are number of factors that influence the course of verbal learning. The most important determinants of verbal learning are the different features of the verbal material to be learned. They include length of the list to be learned and meaningfulness of the material.

Meaningfulness of material is measured in different ways. They are
- Number of associations drawn out in a fixed time.
- Familiarity of the material and frequency of usage.
- Relations among the words in the list.
- Sequential dependence of each word of the list on the preceding words.

Lists of nonsense syllables are available with different levels of associations. The nonsense syllables should be selected from a list containing the same association value. On the basis of research findings, the following generalisations have been made

- Learning time increases with increase in length of the list. A fixed amount of time is necessary to learn a fixed amount of material, regardless of the number of trials into which that time is divided. The more time it takes to learn, the stronger becomes the learning.

- It is found that if participants are not restricted to the serial learning method and are allowed to give free recall, verbal learning becomes organisational. It means participants of free recall method will present words in a new sequence or order compared to original list.

- **Bousfield** did an experiment using list of 60 words which had 15 words each drawn from different cate- gories like names, animals, professions and vegetables.

- However, these words were presented to participants in random order, participants recalled words by organising them in category wise. He called this **category clustering**[4]. It is to be noted that free recall is always organised subjectively i.e. participants organise words or items in their individual ways and recall accordingly.

- Verbal learning is usually intentional, but a person may learn some features of the words unintentionally or incidentally. Verbal learning can be both intentional as well as incidental.

Skill Learning

The learning of a task to give accuracy, speed and performance after a high amount of practice is called skill learning. A skill is defined as the ability to perform some difficult task smoothly and efficiently. For example, driving, airplane piloting, ship navigating, shorthand writing etc. These skill are learned by practice and exercise.

Phases of Skill Learning

Skill learning passes through many phases. With each attempt, the level of skill increases and becomes smoother and less effort demanding. It becomes spontaneous or automatic. In transition from one phase to next, if the level of performance is same, it is called **performance plateau**. In next phase, performance improves and its level goes up.

Fitts conducted experiments to show the phases of skill learning. Skill learning in each phase has different types of mental processes. Skill learning has three phases

- (i) **Cognitive** Learner has to understand and memorise the instructions and understand how to do the task. In this phase, every outside signal, instructional demand and one's response outcome should be kept alive in consciousness.

- (ii) **Associative** In this phase, different sensory inputs (like hearing, seeing, etc) are linked with appropriate responses. As the practice increases, errors decrease, performance improves and time taken is also reduced. Learner has to be attentive to all the sensory inputs and maintain concentration on the task, even though his performance becomes errorless.

- (iii) **Autonomous** There are two important changes in the performance. The attentional demands i.e. being attentive to sensory inputs will decrease and interference created by external factors reduces. Finally, skilled performance gets **automaticity**[5] with minimum demands on conscious effort.

Practice is the only way for skill learning. With increase in practice, there is a gradual increase in improvement rate. Thus, automaticity of errorless performance becomes important feature of the skill.

Factors Facilitating Learning

Some of the most important factors that facilitate learning are

Schedule of Reinforcement Delivery

In learning experiments, we can arrange to deliver reinforcement according to a particular schedule. There are two kinds of schedules for reinforcement. They are **continuous** and **partial reinforcement**.

Continuous Reinforcement

In continuous reinforcement, participant is given reinforcement after every target response. This produces a high rate of responding. But if reinforcement is stopped, response rates will decrease very quickly and the responses obtained under this schedule will tend to reduce and ultimately end.

Partial Reinforcement

In schedules, where reinforcement is not continuous, some responses are not reinforced. Therefore, they are called partial or intermittent reinforcement. Partial reinforcement schedules usually produce very high rates of responding, particularly when responses are reinforced according to ratio.

In this type of schedule, it becomes difficult to tell when a reinforcement has been stopped or just delayed, because an organism makes several responses that are not reinforced.

Thus, it becomes difficult to find out when a reinforcement has been discontinued completely and when it has only been delayed. When reinforcement is continuous it is easier to identify when it has been discontinued. This kind of difference has been found important for extinction. It has been found that extinction of a response is more difficult following partial reinforcement than following continuous reinforcement.

---

4 Category clustering. The mental act of assigning information into categories at the time of recall is known as category clustering.

5 Automaticity When a skill or a task can be carried out or performed easily without conscious effort or intention it is known as automaticity.

The phenomenon that responses acquired under partial reinforcement are highly resistant to extinction which is called **partial reinforcement effect**.

Motivation

It is a mental and physiological state, which excites or provokes an organism to act for fulfilling the present need or future goal. These acts will continue until the goal is achieved and the need is satisfied. Motivation is required as a prior condition for learning.

Motivation for learning comes from two sources.

One is we learn something because we enjoy it, this is called **intrinsic motivation**. The other one comes because they provide the means for achieving some other goal, this is called **extrinsic motivation**.

Preparedness for Learning

Sensory capacities and response abilities are different for members of different species. The processes required to establish associations like S-S (Stimulus-Stimulus) or S-R (Stimulus-Response) are also different for different species. Species have biological limitations on their learning capacities.

The kinds of S-S or S-R learning in an organism depends on its genetical makeup which might facilitate certain associative mechanisms. It means, one can learn only those associations for which one is generically prepared.

Understanding Preparedness

The concept of preparedness might be best understood as a continuum or dimension. **Continuum** refers to a continuous sequence in which adjacent items are not much different from each other but the extreme ends are quite different. On one end, we can keep those tasks or associations which are easy for some species. On other end, those learning tasks are kept which these species cannot learn at all. In the middle, all those tasks are there which can be learnt but with great difficulty and continuous practice.

Learning Disabilities

It is a heterogenous group of disorders which are visible in terms of difficulty in the acquisition of learning, reading, writing, speaking, reasoning and mathematical activities. Sources of such disorders are inherent permanently in the child. These difficulties originate from problems with the functioning of the **Central Nervous System** (CNS).

It may occur along wgith physical handicaps, sensory impairment, intellectual disability or without them.

It should be noted that learning disabilities may be observed as a distinct handicapping condition in children of average to superior intelligence, adequate sensory motor systems, and adequate learning opportunities. If the disability of a child is not remedied on time, it may continue throughout life and affect self-esteem, vocation, social relations, and daily living activities of the child.

Symptoms of Learning Disabilities

Following are some of the symptoms of learning disabilities

- Difficulties in writing letters, words and phrases, reading out text and speaking. Many times childrens have listening problems though they may not have any auditory problems. These children are very different from others in developing learning strategies and plans.

- Disorders of attention, i.e. they get easily distracted and cannot pay attention on one point for long. This lack of attention leads to hyperactivity i.e. they are always moving, doing different things and trying to control things without interruption.

- Poor space orientation and inadequate sense of time are common symptoms. Such children do not get easily adapt to new surroundings and get lost. They are either late or sometimes too early in their routine work. They are confused about direction and misjudge right, left, up and down.

- Learning-disabled children have poor motor co-ordination i.e. poor ability to walk, run, hold objects, etc and poor manual dexterity i.e. poor skill in doing tasks with hands.

- Fail to understand and follow oral directions for doing things.

- Misjudge relationships as to which classmates are friendly and who are not. They fail to learn and understand body language.

- Learning-disabled children usually show perceptual disorders i.e. unable to interpret things. It may be visual, auditory, sense of touch, and kinaesthetic (movement of body parts) misperception. They cannot differentiate between call-bell and telephone ring. They do not have any problem in their sensory organs but they just cannot use it in performance.

- In case of **dyslexia**[6], children usually fail to copy letters and words. They fail to differentiate between p and q, P and 9, was and saw, unclear, and nuclear etc. i.e. fail to organise verbal materials.

- It is noteworthy that learning disabilities are not incurable. Remedial teaching methods help such children in their learning process like other students. Educational psychologists have developed a number of adequate techniques for correcting most of the symptoms related to learning disabilities.

---

6 **Dyslexia** It is a learning disability which involves difficulty in reading, writting, or speaking. It is related to language and speech difficulties wherein a perso finds it difficult to process and understand language.

Chapter Practice

Objective Questions

• Multiple Choice Questions

1. Any relatively permanent change in behaviour or behavioural potential produced by experience is called?
(a) Observation   (b) Learning
(c) Attention   (d) Conditioning

Ans. (b) Learning is the process through which changes in behaviour which are relatively permanent and expands one's knowledge about something.

2. Which of the following are two types of conditioning?
(a) Cognitive learning, and observational learning
(b) Classical conditioning and skill learning
(c) Cognitive learning, and skill learning
(d) Classical conditioning, and operant conditioning

Ans. (d) Classical conditioning and operant conditioning are the two types of conditioning, which are the most simplest type of learning.

3. Who among the following was/were psychologists who demonstrated the phenomenon of Learned helplessness through an experiment on dogs?
(a) Ivan Pavlov   (b) B.F. Skinner
(c) Seligman and Maier   (d) Kohler

Ans. (c) Seligman and Maier were the psychologists who demonstrated the phenomenon of learned helplessness in a study on dogs. This is experienced when after repeated failure and setback, an individual learns to easily give up even when the possibility of success is there.

4. What is the phenomenon of responding similarly to similar stimuli is known as?
(a) Discrimination
(b) Generic process
(c) Generalisation
(d) Spontaneous recovery

Ans. (c) Generalisation is a phenomenon responding similarly to similar stimuli. For example, a child is conditioned to fear all white animals, be it rat or a horse.

5. Among the given options, which of the pairings are correct?
(a) Ivan Pavlov– Operant conditioning
(b) Seligman and Maier– Learned helplessness
(c) B.F Skinner– Classical conditioning
(d) Tolman– Verbal learning

Ans. (b) Seligman and Maier demonstrated learned helplessness in a study on dogs. Therefore, the correct option is (b).

6. A _______ is defined as any stimulus or event, which increases the probability of the occurrence of a (desired) response.
(a) incentive   (b) reward
(c) reinforcer   (d) punishment

Ans. (c) A reinforcer is defined as any stimulus or event which increases the probability of the occurrence of a (desired) response.

7. Learned helplessness underlies psychological cases of _______.
(a) anxiety disorders   (b) eating disorders
(c) depression   (d) bipolar disorder

Ans. (c) Learned helplessness underlies psychological cases of depression.

8. Operant conditioning was investigated by _______.
(a) Tolman   (b) Kohler   (c) Skinner   (d) Pavlov

Ans. (c) Operant conditioning was investigated by Skinner.

9. Consider the following statements and identify the incorrect ones.
(i) Learning involves some kind of experience.
(ii) Learning is only possible through rote learning.
(iii) Behavioural change which occurs due to learning must be relatively permanent.
(iv) Learning is the same as performance.
Options
(a) (i) & (iii)   (b) (i) & (iv)
(c) (ii) & (iii)   (d) (ii) & (iv)

Ans. (d) Learning is not only possible through rote learning, it involves a change which occurs through some experience. So (d) is the correct answer.

10. Choose the correct examples of primary and secondary reinforcers.

(i) Primary reinforcer- money

(ii) Primary reinforcer- water

(iii) Secondary reinforcer- food

(iv) Secondary reinforcer- praise

Options

(a) (i) & (iii)   (b) (i) & (iv)   (c) (ii) & (iii)   (d) (ii) & (iv)

Ans. (d) Primary reinforcers are basic and essential need of human beings for e.g., water whereas, secondary reinforcer is one which has acquired characteristics of the reinforcer for e.g., praise.

11. Consider the following statements about latent learning and choose the correct options.

(i) Latent learning is a type of observational learning.

(ii) Tolman made an early contribution to the concept of latent learning.

(iii) Tolman studied the concept of latent learning by conducting a study on cats.

(iv) Through his experiment, he came to discover something called 'cognitive map.

Options

(a) (i) & (iii)   (b) (ii) & (iv)   (c) (iii) & (iv)   (d) (i) & (iv)

Ans. (b) Tolman conducted a study to understand latent learning, and through his experiment on rats, he discovered the tendency to create mental representation of spatial locations, which he called 'cognitive-maps'. Thus, option (b) is the correct answer.

12. Which of the following is not true about motivation?

(i) Motivation is a mental as well as a physiological state, which arouses an organism to act for fulfilling the current need.

(ii) Motivation is not a prerequisite for learning.

(iii) Two types of motivation are monetary motivation, and spiritual motivation.

(iv) The more motivated you are to succeed, the more hard work you do.

Options

(a) (i) & (iv)   (b) (ii) & (iii)

(c) (iii) & (iv)   (d) (i) & (iii)

Ans. (b) Motivation is a prerequisite for learning. Two types of motivation are intrinsic and extrinsic.

13. A company has found a new way to encourage employees to work hard. They give discount vouchers to employees who overachieve their targets in a week. However, this reward system has seemed to lower employee's __________.

(a) motivation   (b) extrinsic motivation

(c) intrinsic motivation   (d) personal motivation

Ans. (c) Intrinsic motivation is an individual's innate desire to do something that is not influenced by external rewards. Giving rewards for some task which a person likes doing, might hamper his/her intrinsic motivation.

14. 6 year old Hina has a favourite television actress. She watches her shows, advertisements, and videos because she wants to be just like her. She always tries to imitate the actress' mannerisms and way of talking. Hina is engaging in __________ learning.

(a) latent   (b) observational

(c) insight   (d) skill

Ans. (b) Hina is engaging in observational learning. Observational learning involves replication of a behavior after observing it. The little girl is watching and imitating the behaviour of an actress. Hence, the correct option is (b).

• Assertion-Reasoning MCQs

Directions (Q. Nos. 1-4) *Each of these questions contains two statements, Assertion (A) and Reason (R). Each of these questions also has four alternative choices, any one of which is the correct answer. You have to select one of the codes (a), (b), (c) and (d) given below.*

(a) Both A and R are true and R is the correct explanation of A

(b) Both A and R are true, but R is not the correct explanation of A

(c) A is true and R is false

(d) A is false and R is true

1. Assertion (A) Sometimes behavioural change happens in people who are on sedatives or drugs or alcohol.

Reason (R) Such changes are permanent and lead to learning.

Ans. (c) Sometimes changes in behaviour happens in people who are on drugs due to physiological effects and are of temporary nature and not permanent so Assertion (A) is true and Reason (R) is false.

2. Assertion (A) One learns to put on woolen clothes to avoid the unpleasant cold weather.

Reason (R) In Positive reinforcement people take action which is followed by a positive outcome.

Ans. (b) One learn to put on woollen clothes to avoid the unpleasant cold weather is an instance of negative reinforcement. In negative reinforcement, an individual will take action to escape or avoid something negative, on the other hand, in positive reinforcement, people take action because it is followed by a positive outcome.

3. Assertion (A) There is a marked improvement in a person's golf skills from the first day they started to a year later.

Reason (R) Skill learning involves different phases. With each successive attempt at learning a skill, one's performance becomes smoother and less effort demanding.

Ans. (a) Skill learning is a progressive process in which consistent practice leads to efficient performance. Therefore, a person golf skills improvement men more and more practice. Thus, Both A and R are true and R is the correct explanation of A.

4. Assertion (A) It is impossible that a solution to a problem can suddenly become clear.

Reason (R) Insight learning is the type of learning in which the solution to a problem suddenly becomes clear.

Ans. (d) It is possible that sometimes, solutions to a problem can appear suddenly. In a normal experiment on insight learning, a problem is presented, followed by a period of time when no apparent progress is made and finally a solution suddenly emerges. Thus, A is false and R is true.

• Case Based MCQs

1. Read the case and answer the questions that follow.

A scientist wanted to see how a child learns to fear something. For this he conducted an experiment on a child. In the initial trial, he exposed the child to a white rat to see the child's response. But, the child did not react to the rat in any extreme way. There was no fear in the child towards the rat.

In the next trial, the child was again exposed to a white rat but this time it was immediately followed by an extremely loud bang. The child's immediate response was that of shock, fear, and crying. This happened a few times and in the third trial, only the rat was presented in front of the child without the loud bang. The child starts to cry every time he sees the rat.

In the last trial, the experimenter exposed the child to different white animals, such as birds or cats. It was observed that the child started showing fear towards other white creatures besides white rats.

(i) Identify the kind of learning in this experiment?
(a) Classical Conditioning
(b) Operant Conditioning
(c) Latent learning
(d) Delayed Reinforcement

Ans. (a) In this experiment child learns to associate fear with white rat through classical conditioning. Classical conditioning is a learning theory developed by Ivan Pavlov.

(ii) Identify the neutral stimulus prior to conditioning in this experiment?
(a) Loud and scary sounds   (b) White rat
(c) Other fuzzy white objects
(d) Scientist himself

Ans. (b) In this experiment, the neutral stimulus is the white rat because it did not create any response on its own. Hence, it was neutral. Only after being paired with the loud noise it became the conditioned stimulus.

(iii) Who among the following scientists first investigated Classical Conditioning?
(a) Ivan P Pavlov   (b) Albert Bandura
(c) Wolfgang Kohler   (d) BF Skinner

Ans. (a) Ivan P. Pavlov is regarded as the pioneer of classical conditioning. His famous experiment on dogs lead to the establishment of classical conditioning theory.

(iv) Two statements are given in the question below as Assertion (A) and Reasoning (R). Read the statements and choose the appropriate option.

Assertion (A) The loud bang noise causes the child to cry and become fearful.

Reason (R) Because the loud bang is a conditioned stimulus.

Options
(a) Both A and R are true, and R is the correct explanation of A
(b) Both A and R are true, but R is not the correct explanation of A
(c) A is true, R is false
(d) A is false, R is true

Ans. (c) The loud noise generates fear and anxiety in a child because it is an unconditioned stimulus. This type of stimulus creates a response which is natural and is not artificially created. Thus, A is true and R is false.

(v) In the experiment the child responded with fear to other white animals. This phenomenon of responding similarly to similar stimuli is known as ________.
(a) conditioning   (b) generalisation
(c) discrimination   (d) extinction

Ans. (b) Generalisation is the type of conditioning in which one learns to react to similar stimuli in the same way. One fears all birds equally and not just one type. This is an example of generalisation.

(vi) What is the unconditioned response in this experiment?
(a) Loud bang   (b) Fear and crying
(c) No reaction   (d) White rat

Ans. (b) The unconditioned response in this experiment is fear and crying because. Unconditioned response is the type of response which is natural and happens without any manipulations. Therefore, fear is a natural response to a loud noise, which makes it the unconditioned response.

Subjective Questions

• Short Answer (SA) Type Questions

1. Discuss about how psychologists conduct learning experiments to know how a list of words is learned.

Ans. Learning involves a series of psychological events. This can be understood using a learning experiment. Suppose psychologists wanted to know about how a list of words is learned. They will conduct a series of experiments in the following consequences

- Do a pre-test to know how much the person knows before learning.
- Present the list of words to be remembered for a fixed time.
- The list of words is processed towards acquiring new knowledge.
- After processing is complete, new knowledge is acquired and information is recalled by the persons.

Now psychologists will compare the number of words which a person has newly learnt compared to what she/he knows before the test. By doing this, they will infer that learning did take place.

2. Discuss about the classical conditioning procedures based on time relations between stimuli.

Ans. There are basically four types of classical conditioning procedures. They are based on the time relations between the beginning of Conditioned Stimulus (CS) and Unconditioned Stimulus (US).

The first three are called forward conditioning procedures, and the fourth one is called backward conditioning procedure. Following are the basic experimental arrangements of these procedures

- When the CS and US are started together, it is called simultaneous conditioning.
- When CS is started first before the start of US and CS ends first before the end of US, it is called delayed conditioning.
- When CS starts and ends before the start of US, and if there is a time gap between the two, it is called trace conditioning. Explain how she gets motivated to study.
- When US comes before the start of CS, it is called backward conditioning.

3. Explain Skinner experiment with respect to operant conditioning.

Ans. Skinner conducted his studies on rats and pigeons in specially made boxes called Skinner Box. One hungry rat is placed inside the box such that it could not come out but just move inside the box.

A lever which was connected to a food container was kept at the top of the chamber. While moving around which is called exploratory behaviour, the rat accidentally presses the lever and a food pellet drops on the plate, and the hungry rat eats it. In next trial, after a while the exploratory behaviour again starts and this continues.

As number of trials increases, the time taken to press the lever by the rat for the food decreases. Conditioning is complete when rat presses the lever immediately after it is kept in the chamber. In this scenario, lever pressing is an operant response and getting food is its consequence. As the response is instrumental in getting the food, this type of learning is called instrumental conditioning.

4. Discuss about Bousfield experiment.

Ans. This Bousfield did this experiment in 1953 using a list of 60 words which had 15 words each drawn from different categories like names, animals, professions and vegetables. When these words were presented to participants in random order, participants recalled words by organising them in categorywise.

He called this category clustering. Free recall is always organised subjectively i.e. participants organise words or items in their individual ways and recall accordingly. Participants notice features like two or more words rhyming, starting with identical letters, having same vowels, etc.

5. Pooja is studying seriously to get good marks in her final exam. Explain how she gets motivated to study.

Ans. Pooja is studying seriously, as she wants to pass with good marks or grades in her final examination. She is a motivated student and does hard work for learning. Her motivation for learning or study arises from two sources. She learns her subjects because she enjoys them. It is her intrinsic motivation. Again she learns subjects for attaining some other goal. It is her extrinsic motivation. May be she wants to become an engineer or doctor. This motivation makes her to study seriously.

6. "Many of the children join schools but drop-out because some of them find the demands of educational process very difficult." Justify the statement.

Ans. There are some reasons of the children who join schools but drop-out are as follows

- We have heard, observed or read that thousands of children get enrolled for education in schools. Some of them however, find the demands of educational process too difficult to meet, and they drop out such students are called 'dropouts'.
- There are many reasons for this drop-out like sensory impairment, intellectual disability, social and emotional disturbance, poor economic conditions of the family, cultural beliefs and norms or other environmental influences.

- Other than these reasons there is another important source of problem in the path of education, that is called learning disabilities.
- It makes school learning i.e. obtaining knowledge and skill very difficult.
- Such children also fail to move forward in their learning activities.
- Sometimes students with learning disabilities also cannot continue their study in schools. Often they get easily distracted and cannot pay attention. They fail to understand and follow oral directions for doing things.
- Students with dyslexia quite often fail to copy letters and words. For all these reasons students dropout from the school.

7. Discuss about types of unconditioned stimuli in studying classical conditioning.

Ans. There are two types of unconditioned stimuli used in studying classical conditioning. They are

(i) **Appetitive** This stimuli automatically draws out approach responses like eating, drinking, caressing, etc. It means these kind of events will make us feel good and we would love to participate in such events.

These kind of responses give satisfaction and pleasure. Appetitive classical conditioning is slower and it requires large number of acceptance trials.

(ii) **Aversive** This stimuli like noise, bitter taste, electric shock, painful injections, etc are painful, harmful and draws out avoidance and escape responses. Aversive classical conditioning is established in one, two or three trials depending on the intensity of the aversive Unconditioned Stimulus (US).

8. List different scenarios that affect the resistance to extinction.

Ans. Different scenarios affecting resistance to extinction which are as follows.

- Resistance to extinction increases and learned response reaches its highest level and performance gets stabilised, when number of reinforced trials are increased. Hereafter, response strength is not affected by number of trials.
- Resistance to extinction increases when number of reinforcements are increased during acquisition trials. After a point, if we increase number of reinforcements, the resistance to extinction decreases.
- Resistance to extinction increases if reinforcement is delayed during acquisition trials. Continuous reinforcement makes the learned response to be less resistant to extinction and more in case of partial reinforcement.

9. Discuss about learned helplessness.

Ans. Learned helplessness occurs when people or animals feel helpless to avoid negative situations. It is one of the causes for depression.

Seligman and Maier conducted experiments on dogs to demonstrate this phenomenon. In first part, dogs were subjected to sound (conditioned stimulus) and electric shock (unconditioned stimulus) using classical conditioning procedure. There was no scope for dogs to escape shock.

After repeated trials, they were subjected to shock in an operant conditioning procedure, in which dogs could escape shock by pressing their head against wall. But dog just suffered the shock and did not attempt to escape. This behaviour of dog was called learned helplessness.

10. List the differences between classical and operant conditioning.

Ans. Differences between classical and operant conditioning are as follows

Classical	Operant
Responses are under control of some stimulus because they are automatically given by the appropriate stimuli.	Responses are under control of the organism and are voluntary responses or operants.
Conditioned stimulus (CS) and unconditioned stimulus(US) are well defined.	CS is not defined. It can be just inferred, not directly known.
Experimenter controls the occurrence of US. Organism remains passive.	The occurrence of the reinforcer is under the control of the organism i.e. learning. Subject is active in order to be reinforced.

11. A good role model is very important for a growing up child. Discuss the kind of learning that supports it.   **(NCERT)**

Ans. A good role model is very important for a growing up child and that good role model can be anyone, be it father, mother or some great people from the society like Abdul Kalam, Mother Teresa, etc. It is important because a child will try to observe others and try to imitate their behaviour. This kind of learning is helped by observational learning.

In this type, learning happens by observing others. It was earlier called imitation. Bandura and his colleagues studied observational learning in detail. It is also called **social learning** because humans learn social behaviour through this. Individuals try to emulate the behaviour of others in many situations and this is called modeling.

12. Explain the study of Bandura with respect to observational learning.

Ans. Bandura conducted an experimental study in which he has shown a movie of five minute duration to children. The film has a large room with number of toys including a large sized Bobo doll.

Now a grown-up boy enters the room. Boy shows aggressive behaviour towards toys and he hits the bobo doll, throws it on the floor, kicking it and sitting on it. This film has three versions, children were shown. These were

(i) That the boy (model) was rewarded for being aggressive.

(ii) That the boy was punished for being aggressive.

(iii) That the boy was neither punished nor rewarded.

Now when children were kept in a similar room with toys, children behaved differently i.e. children who saw boy being awarded behaved in most aggressive manner and children who saw boy being punished behaved in least aggressive manner.

Thus, in observational learning observers get knowledge by observing model's behaviour, but performance is influenced by model's behaviour being rewarded or punished.

Children learn most of the social behaviours by observing and emulating adults. Aggressiveness, pro-social behaviour, courtesy, politeness, diligence, laziness are acquired by this method of learning.

13. Explain the Kohler experiment.

Ans. Kohler conducted experiments with chimpanzees to demonstrate insight learning. He placed chimpanzees in an enclosed play area where food was kept outside their reach.

They were provided with some boxes and poles. Chimpanzees very soon learnt how to use these boxes and poles to get the food. They did not do it by trial and error method, but all of a sudden, they would stand on a box and use a pole to strike a banana.

This kind of learning is called insight learning i.e. a sudden solution to the problem. Once the solution is found, it can be repeated immediately the next time the problem appears. So, this learning is not the result of a specific set of conditioned stimuli and responses but a cognitive relationship between a means and an end (goal). Thus, insight learning can be generalised to other similar problems.

• Long Answer (LA) Type Questions

1. Discuss about different key processes of learning.

Ans. Learning is a psychological process which gradually develops in human being.

There are different processes that are involved in learning through either classical or operant conditioning. These are discussed as follows

Reinforcement It is the activity of managing a reinforcer by the experimenter. Reinforcers are agents that increase the rate of the responses that come ahead. Reinforced responses increase in rate and non-reinforced responses decrease in rate.

Extinction It means disappearance of a learned response due to removal of reinforcement from the situation in which the response used to occur. Learning shows resistance to extinction, it means even if learned response is not reinforced, it would continue for sometime.

Generalisation and Discrimination The phenomenon of responding similarly to similar stimuli is known as generalisation. Discrimination is a response due to difference. Discriminative response depends on the discrimination capacity or discrimination learning of the organism.

Spontaneous Recovery It occurs after a learned response has ended. It has been shown that after lapse of considerable time, the learned or conditioned response recovers and occurs to the conditioned stimulus.

The amount of spontaneous recovery depends on the duration of the time lapsed after the extinction session. Recovery of the learned response is stronger if the duration of time lapse is longer and such a recovery occurs spontaneously.

2. List out the differences between analytic and relational style of learning.

Ans. Anderson recognised difference between analytic and relational styles of learning as follows

Analytical Style	Relational Style
In this style of learning people are able to break information from total picture and focus on detail.	In this style of learning people interpret information as part of total picture.
This style of learning shows sequential and structured thinking.	This style of learning shows intuitive thinking i.e. based on feelings.
This type of learning style has learn materials that are inanimate and impersonal more easily.	This type of learning style has learn materials that have a human, social content and are described by experiential/cultural relevance more easily.
People who learn through this learning style have a good memory for abstract (theoretical) ideas and irrelevant information.	People who learn through this learning style have a good memory for verbally presented ideas and information, especially if relevant.
People after using this style of learning are more task-oriented in connection with academics.	People after using this style of learning are more task-oriented in connection to non-academic areas.
People who acquired this learning style are not greatly affected by the opinions of others.	People who acquired this learning style are Influenced by authority figures, expression of confidence or doubt in students ability.

3. What is learning? What are its distinguishing features?

Ans. Learning may be defined as "any relatively permanent change in behaviour or behavioural potential produced by experience". It refers to a range of changes that take place as a result of one's experience. There are different features for the proscess of learning. These are discussed as follows

   (i) **Learning by Experience** We experience an event occurring in a certain sequence during different occasions. If an event happens then it might be followed by some other events. If some action is repeatedly done and if it gives satisfaction, this experience will lead to the formation of habit.

   (ii) **Temporary Behavioural Changes** In the process of learning, behavioural changes that occur due to learning are relatively permanent. Changes in behaviour might occur due to the effects of tiredness, repeated monotonous work and drugs.

   (iii) **Learning Involves Sequence of Psychological Events** Psychologists suggest that learning process always needs a series of psychological events on consecutive sequences, viz, a pre-test to know the extent of learning, list of words to be remembered, after processing information is to be recalled etc.

   (iv) **Learning is an Inferred Process and is Different from Performance** When a student recites a poem, he gives his performance. By seeing his performance the teacher infers that now learning took place which was not done by the student previously.

4. How does classical conditioning demonstrate learning by association? **(NCERT)**

Ans. Classical conditioning is also known as respondent conditioning. It is a learning procedure in which a biological agent like food is paired with a neutral agent like bell. In this, a new behaviour is learnt *via* the process of association.

Learning by association can be understood through the following experiment of Pavlov

Experiment of Pavlov Ivan P Pavlov was the first one to experiment this type of learning. Pavlov designed an experiment using dog to understand this process. He observed that dogs secreted saliva whenever they saw the plate in which they were served food. In the first part of the experiment, a dog was kept in the box to conduct experiment.

A simple surgery was conducted, and one end of a tube was inserted in the dog's jaw and the other end of tube was put in a measuring glass. This was used to measure the amount of saliva dog secreted. In the second part of the experiment, the dog was kept hungry and placed in harness. A bell was rang and immediately after the sound, food (meat powder) was served to dog. The dog was allowed to eat it.

This routine was continued for next few days i.e immediately after ringing the bell, food was given to the dog. After a number of such trials, a test trail was conducted in which, everything was repeated except that food was not served to dog after ringing the bell. The dog still secreted saliva after listening to the sound of the bell, expecting its food to be served, because dog thought bell and food were connected. This connection between bell and food resulted in obtaining a new response by the dog, i.e secreting saliva to the sound of bell. This has been called conditioning.

5. Define operant conditioning. Discuss the factors that influence the course of operant conditioning. **(NCERT)**

Ans. Operant conditioning is a learning process through which strength of the behaviour is modified by reward or punishment. The factors that influence the course of operant conditioning are:

   (i) **Types of Reinforcement** Reinforcement may be positive or negative. Positive reinforcement has agents that have pleasant consequences and thus strengthen and maintain the responses. Food, water, medals, praise, money, status, information, etc are positive reinforcers which satisfy needs. Negative reinforcers has unpleasant and painful agents. Thus, negative reinforcement leads to learning of avoidance and escape responses.

   (ii) **Number of Reinforcement and Other Features** It refers to the number of trials after which an organism is reinforced or rewarded. Amount of reinforcement means how much food or water or intensity of pain causing agent is used as reinforcing stimulus or agent for each trial. Reinforcers like chick-peas or pieces of bread compared to raisins or pieces of cake are inferior in quality. This refers to quality of reinforcement.

   (iii) **Schedules of Reinforcement** It refers to the arrangement of the delivery of reinforcement during conditioning trials. Reinforcement given in every trial or in some trials i.e. it may be continuous or intermittent (partial). In continuous reinforcement, desire response is reinforced every time and in partial reinforcement, responses may or may not get reinforced. Partial reinforcement produces greater resistance to extinction.

   (iv) **Delayed Reinforcement** Delay in the delivery of reinforcement leads to decrease in the level of performance.

6. How can we identify students with learning disabilities?

Ans. Learning disabilities cause difficulty in the acquisition of learning, reading, writing, speaking, reasoning, and mathematical activities. The various symptoms of learning disabilities are

- Difficulties in writing letters, words and phrases, reading out text and speaking quite frequently appear. Many times they have listening problems though they may not have any auditory problems. These children are very different from others in developing learning strategies and plans.
- Disorders of attention, i.e. they get easily distracted and cannot pay attention on one point for long. This lack of attention leads to hyperactivity i.e. they are always moving, doing different things and trying to control things without interruption.
- Poor body postures, inadequate knowledge about one's own space and inadequate sense of time are common symptoms. Such children do not get easily adapt to new surroundings and get lost. They are either late or sometimes too early in their routine work. They are confused about direction and misjudge right, left, up and down.
- Poor motor coordination i.e. poor ability to walk, run, hold objects, etc and poor manual dexterity i.e. poor skill in doing tasks with hands.
- This we can see in children with their lack of balance, inability to sharpen pencil, handle doorknobs, unable to learn ride bicycle, etc.
- Perceptual disorders i.e. unable to interpret things. It may be visual, auditory, sense of touch, and kinaesthetic (movement of body parts) misperception. They can not differentiate between call bell and telephone ring. They do not have any problem in their sensory organs but they just can not use it in performance.
- Dyslexia i.e. children usually fail to copy letters and words. They fail to differentiate between p and q, P and 9, was and saw, unclear, and nuclear etc. i.e. fail to organise verbal materials.

7. Elaboratel the different factors that facilitate learning.

Ans. Some of the important factors that facilitating learning are as follows

- **Schedule of Reinforcement Delivery** In learning experiments, we can arrange to deliver reinforcement according to a particular schedule. There are two kinds of schedules for reinforcement. They are **continuous** and **partial reinforcement**.
- **Motivation** It is a mental and physiological state, which excites or provokes an organism to act for fulfilling the present need or future goal. These acts will continue until the goal is achieved and the need is satisfied. Motivation is required as a prior condition for learning.

  Motivation for learning comes from two sources. One is we learn something because we enjoy it, this is called **intrinsic motivation**.

The other one comes because they provide the means for achieving some other goal, this is called **extrinsic motivation**.

- **Preparedness for Learning** Sensory capacities and response abilities are different for members of different species. The processes required to establish associations like S-S (Stimulus-Stimulus) or S-R (Stimulus-Response) are also different for different species. Species have biological limitations on their learning capacities.

  The kinds of S-S or S-R learning in an organism depends on its genetical makeup which might facilitate certain associative mechanisms. It means, one can learn only those associations for which one is generically prepared.

• Case Based Questions

1. Read the case and answer the questions that follow.

In an experiment, a scientist divided participants into three groups. One group was subjected to a loud and unpleasant noise but was able to terminate the noise by pressing a button four times; the second group was subjected to the same noise, but the button was not functional; and the third group was subjected to no noise at all.

Later, all the participants were subjected to a loud noise and given a box with a lever which, when manipulated, would turn off the sound. In this experiment, those who had no control over the noise in the first part of the experiment generally did not even try to turn the noise off, while the rest of the subjects generally figured out how to turn the noise off very quickly.

(i) Identify the psychological phenomenon that has been demonstrated in the given experiment.

Ans. In the given experiment Learned helplessness has been demonstrated. It was introduced by Martin Seligman and Maier.It suggests that continuous failure in a set of tasks shows the occurrence of learned helplessness.

(ii) Who among the following scientists first investigated the phenomenon given in the passage?

Ans. Martin Seligman and Maier were the first scientists who demonstrated the phenomenon of learned helplessness in a study on dogs.

(iii) According to the experiment, what leads to helplessness?

Ans. According to the experiment, continuous failure leads to helplessness. An individual learns to give up more easily because he or she has faced continuous and persistent setbacks and failures.

2. Refer to the picture given below and answer the questions by choosing the most appropriate option.

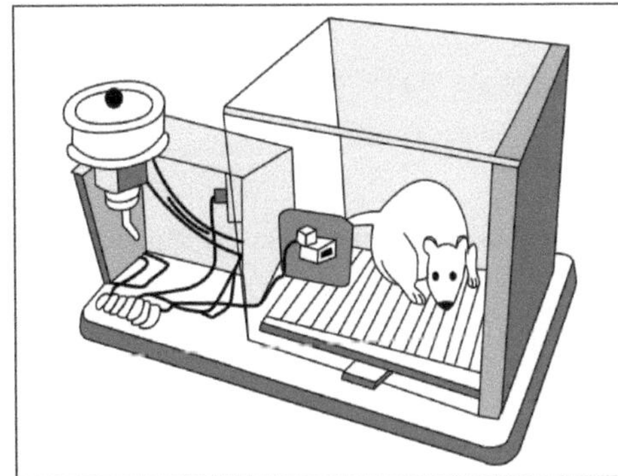

(i) Identify the name of the instrument used in this experiment?

Ans. B.F. Skinner conducted his studies on rats and pigeons in specially made boxes, called the Skinner Box

(ii) Which psychologist conducted experiments on rats to study the occurrence of voluntary responses when an organism operates on the environment?

Ans. Operant conditioning was first investigated by B.F. Skinner. Skinner studied occurrence of voluntary responses when an organism operates on the environment.

(iii) In this experiment, the rats learn that lever pressing is an operant response and getting food is its consequence explain.

Ans. In this experiment, the rat presses the lever faster after it was rewarded with food. With trial the rat presses the lever more quickly. The conditioning is complete when the rat presses the lever immediately after it is placed in the chamber. Thus, getting food is the consequence.

3. Read the case and answer the questions that follow.

A scientist wanted to see how dogs learn new behaviours. The scientist conducted this experiment in a laboratory where the dog was kept.

There were two rooms connected to the main room where the dog was kept. One of the rooms had food which the dogs like to eat but the entrance of the room was blocked by a big wooden board.

The scientist wanted to see how the dog would get to the other side and reach the food. In the initial phase the dog restlessly stayed before the board, not knowing how to reach the food. Then after some time, out of the blue, the dog pushed the wooden board with his front legs and went inside the room and ate the food. The solution comes out of nowhere without trying or making any effort.

In the next trial, it took no time for the dog to push the board to go inside the room. The dog had learned that by pushing the door he could go inside.

(i) Which theory of learning is being demonstrated in this experiment and who was its pioneer?

Ans. In the given experiment insight theory is being demonstrated. In this experiment, the dog was exposed to a new problem. Through insight, the dog learns that he can get inside the room by pushing the board. This happened without any trial-and-errors. The pioneer of insight learning was Kohler.

(ii) Define insight learning with an example.

Ans. Insight learning involves a process through which the answer to a problem suddenly becomes clear. For example, while playing a video game, a player gets stuck on a particular stage. Then suddenly, the player tries a different technique and succeeds.

(iii) How is insight learning different from observational learning?

Ans. In insight learning, the answer or solution does not come from observing or imitating someone else's actions, rather it comes from an individual's own insight. Insight is sudden and does not involve trial-and-error. Whereas, observational learning is a type of learning which occurs due to observation and imitation.

Chapter Test

Multiple Choice Questions

1. The phenomenon that responses acquired under partial reinforcement are highly resistant to extinction is called ______ effect.
   - (a) Partial reinforcement
   - (b) Continuous reinforcement
   - (c) Positive reinforcement
   - (d) Negative reinforcement

2. ______ means disappearance of a learned response due to removal of reinforcement from the situation in which the response used to occur.
   - (a) Resistance
   - (b) Extinction
   - (c) Discrimination
   - (d) Generalization

3. The set of features that are connected by some rule are called ______ features.
   - (a) Conjunctive
   - (b) Relevant
   - (c) Natural
   - (d) Artificial

4. ______ refers to the preferences of persons through which they take in information such as auditory, visual, smell, kinesthetic, and tactile.
   - (a) Information Processing
   - (b) Personality Patterns
   - (c) Perceptual Modality
   - (d) Learning style

Short Answer (SA) Type Questions

5. Who are Pavlov and Skinner?
6. Define the term learned helplessness.
7. Define perceptual modality.
8. Briefly explain the nature of learning.
9. Describe primary and secondary reinforcers with examples.
10. List the differences between Classical and Operant conditioning.
11. Discuss about Bandura's experiment on observational learning.
12. Define and explain serial learning.
13. Mention the different phases of skill acquisition.

Long Answer (LA) Type Questions

14. What are the symptoms of learning disabilities?
15. Explain briefly the applications of learning principles.
16. Describe the factors which facilitate learning.

Answers

1. (a)   *2.* (b)   *3.* (a)   *4.* (c)

Human Memory

In this Chapter...

Introduction

The first systematic research on memory was done by a German psychologist **Hermann Ebbinghaus** in 1885. He carried out many experiments on himself and found that we do not forget the learned material at an even pace or completely. In the beginning, the rate of memory loss is fast but later it stabilises. **Fredrick Bartlett** (1932) observed that memory is not passive but an active process. Using verbal materials (like stories and texts) he showed that memory is a constructive process. This means, the things we memorise and store undergo many changes and modifications over time.

Nature of Memory

Memory refers to storing and recalling information over a period of time, depending upon the nature of cognitive (mental activities) task you are required to perform.

Memory is conceptualised as a process consisting of three independent but interrelated stages. These are **encoding**, **storage** and **retrieval** which are discussed as follows

Encoding

It is the first stage of memory which refers to a process by which information is recorded and registered for the first time so that it becomes usable by our memory system. Whenever an external stimulus impacts on our sensory organs, it generates neural impulse i.e. the way nerve cells communicate with one another. These are received in different areas of our brain for further processing. In this stage, incoming information is received and some meaning is derived. Then, it represented in a way so that it can be processed further.

Storage

It is the second stage of memory. It is a process through which information is retained and held over a period of time. The information is stored so that it can be put to use later.

Retrieval

Retrieval is the third stage of memory. It refers to bringing the stored information to her/his awareness so that it can be used for performing various cognitive tasks like problem solving and decision-making.

Memory failure can happen at any of the above stages. We may fail to recall an information because, we did not encode it properly or storage was weak and thus, we could not recall it when required.

Information Processing Approach: The Stage Model

Initially, it was believed that human memory is the capacity to store all information (knowledge, facts and memories) that we acquire through learning and experience. Human memory was seen as a vast storehouse where all information that we knew was stored so that we could retrieve and use it as and when needed. But with the coming of computers, human memory came to be seen as a system that processes information in the same way a computer does.

Both of them register, store and manipulate information and act as per the outcome of such manipulations. In computer, we have temporary memory (Random Access Memory or RAM) and a permanent memory (e.g. Hard disk). Based on the programme commands, the computer performs corresponding operations and shows output on the screen.

Similarly, human beings too register information, store and manipulate the stored information depending on the task that they need to perform. For example, when you required to solve a mathematical problem, the memory relating to mathematical operations, such as division or subtraction are carried out, activated and put to use, and receive, the output (the problem solution). This analogy led to the development of the first model of memory, which was proposed by Atkinson and Shiffrin in 1968. It is known as **Stage Model**.

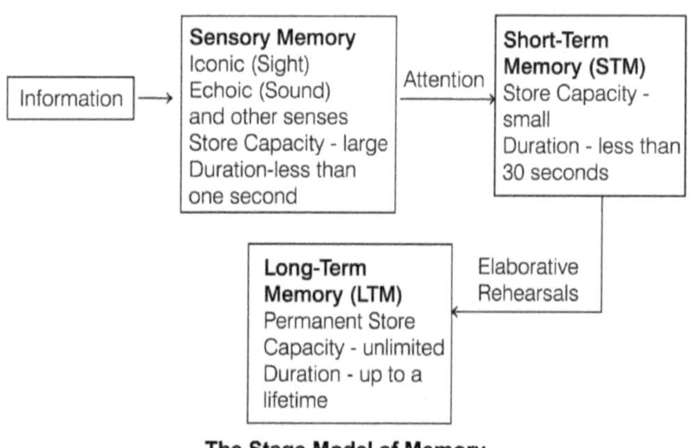

The Stage Model of Memory

Memory Systems

According to the Stage Model, there are three memory systems; the **Sensory Memory**, the **Short-Term Memory** and the **Long-Term Memory**. Each of these systems have different features and perform different functions with respect to the sensory inputs. These are discussed as follows

Sensory Memory

The incoming information first enters sensory memory. It has large capacity but is of very short duration i.e. less than a second. It registers information from each of the senses with reasonable accuracy. This system is referred as sensory memories or sensory registers, because informations from all the senses are registered here as exact replica (copy) of the stimulus. For example, seeing visual after-images i.e. the trial of light that stays after the bulb is switched off and hearing reverberations of a sound after the sound has stopped. These are iconic (visual) or echoic (auditory) sensory registers.

Short-Term Memory (STM)

Information to which attention is payed enters the second memory store called the Short-Term Memory (STM). It holds small amount of information for a brief period of time (usually for 30 seconds or less).

Atkinson and Shiffrin proposed that information in STM is usually **encoded acoustically**[1], i.e. in terms of sound and unless practised continuously, it may get lost from the STM in less than 30 seconds. STM is fragile but not as fragile as sensory registers where the information decays automatically in less than a second.

Long-Term Memory (LTM)

Information that survive the capacity and duration limitations of STM finally enter the Long-Term Memory (LTM). It is a permanent storehouse of all informations that may include very recent incidents or very distant events that might happened 10 years back. It has been shown that once any information enters LTM, it is never forgotten. The reason for this is that information gets encoded logically or meaningfully i.e. in terms of the meaning that any information carries.

Information travels from one memory store to another in the following ways

Control Processes

Atkinson and **Shiffrin** proposed the idea of **control processes** which function to monitor the flow of information through various memory stores. All the information that is received by our senses is not registered. Only that information which is attended to enter the STM from sensory registers,

---

1 **Encoded Acoustically** It is the process of remembering and comprehending something that you hear.

i.e. selective attention. It is the first control process that decides what will travel from sensory registers to STM. Information that does not receive attention fades away quickly.

Maintenance Rehearsal

The STM then sets into motion another control process of **maintenance rehearsal** to retain the information for as much time as required. These kinds of rehearsals simply maintain information through repetition and when such repetitions discontinue the information is lost.

Chunking

Another control process in STM which is used to expand its capacity. For example, if you are told to remember a string of digits like 194719492004, you may create the chunks as 1947, 1949 and 2004 and can easily remember. With help of this method we can remember the important dates of history or current affairs.

Elaborative Rehearsals

From the STM, information enters LTM through **elaborative rehearsals**. In this rehearsal, it attempts to connect the 'to be retained information' to the already existing information in long-term memory. For example, the task of remembering the meaning of word 'humanity' will be easier if the meanings of concepts such as 'compassion', 'truth' and 'benevolence' are already in place.

The number of associations we can create around the new information will determine its permanence.

Experiments, which were done to test the stage model of memory, have produced mixed results. While some experiments unequivocally show that the STM and LTM are indeed two separate memory stores, other evidences have questioned their distinctiveness.

For example, previously it was shown that in the STM information is encoded acoustically, while in LTM it is encoded semantically. But later experimental evidences show that information can also be encoded semantically in STM and acoustically in LTM.

It involves arrangement of the incoming information in as many ways as possible. In the year 1970 *Shallice* and *Warrington* suggested that a man known as 'KF' met with an accident and damaged a portion of the left side of his cerebral hemisphere. It was found that his long- term memory was intact, but the short-term memory was seriously affected.

The stage model suggests that information is committed to the long-term memory via STM and if KF's STM was affected, how can his long-term memory be normal?

Several other studies have also shown that memory processes are similar irrespective of whether any information is retained for a few seconds or for many years and that memory can be adequately understood without positing separate memory stores. All these evidences led to the development of another conceptualisation about memory.

Types of Long-Term Memory (LTM)

As we have seen, the short-term memory is now consisting of more than one component (**working memory**[2]). In the same way it is suggested that long-term memory too is not unitary because it contains a wide variety of information. In view of this contemporary formulations envisage long-term memory as consisting of various types.

The two major classification within the LTM are **declarative** and **procedural memories**. These levels are described as follows

Declarative Memory

All information related to facts, names, dates etc are part of declarative memory. Facts stored in the declarative memory are responsible to verbal descriptions. **Tulving** classified that declarative memory can either be **episodic memory** or **semantic memory**.

Episodic Memory It contains biographical details of our lives. Memories related to our personal life experiences are part of the episodic memory and thats why its contents are generally emotional in nature.

Semantic Memory It contains general awareness and knowledge. All concepts, ideas and rules of logic are stored in semantic memory. Since, the contents of semantic memory relate to facts and ideas of general awareness and knowledge, it is affect-neutral and not susceptible to forgetting.

Procedural Memory

It refers to memories relating to procedures for achieving different tasks and skills like how to ride a bicycle, play football, etc. The contents of procedural memory cannot be described easily. For example, if someone asked you how do you ride a bicycle, you may find it difficult to narrate.

---

2 **Working Memory** It is a cognitive system with a limited capacity that is responsible for temporarily holding information available for processing.

Classification of Long-Term Memory (LTM)

Psychologists have classified LTM into different types. The following phenomena show the complex and dynamic nature of human memory.

Flashbulb Memories

These are memories of events that are very interesting or surprising. These memories are like images frozen in memory and tied to particular places, dates and times. People put in greater effort in the formation of these memories and highlighting details might lead to deeper levels of processing as well as offer more cues for retrieval.

Autobiographical Memory

These are personal memories which are not distributed evenly throughout our lives. Some periods in our lives produce more memories than others. For example, we do not have any memory of our early childhood till 4 to 5 years.

This is called **childhood amnesia**. Just after early adulthood i.e. in the twenties, there is a sudden increase in the frequency of memories. This might be due to emotionality, the quality and importance of events that contribute to it. During old age, the most recent years of life are likely to be well remembered. Around 30 years of age, decline in certain kinds of memory starts.

Implicit Memory

It is a kind of memory that a person is not aware of. It is a memory that is retrieved automatically. Implicit memories lie outside the boundaries of awareness i.e. we are not aware of the fact that a memory or record of a given experience exists. However, implicit memories do influence our behaviour.

This kind of memory was also found in patients suffering from brain injuries. For example, patients were presented a list of common words. A few minutes later a patient was asked to recall words from the list.

No memory was shown for the words. However, if she/he was prompted to say a word that begins with these letters and two letters are given, the patient was able to recall words. Implicit memories are also seen in people with normal memories.

Methods of Memory Measurement

Memory is measured experimentally through a number of ways. Since, we have different kinds of memories, any method appropriate for studying one type of memory may not be suited for studying another. The following are the major methods used for memory measurement

Free Recall and Recognition In free recall method, participants are given some words and are asked to memorise and recall them in any order. The more they are able to recall, the better their memory becomes. In recognition, participants see the items that they had memorised along with distracter items (those that they had not seen) and their task is to identify which one of those they had learnt. The more the number of recognition of old items, the better is the memory.

Sentence Verification Task It is used for measuring semantic memory. We have read that semantic memory is not responsible for any forgetting because it contains general knowledge that we all have. The participants are asked to indicate whether the given sentences are true or false. Faster the participants respond, the better the information needed to verify those sentences is retained.

Priming It is used for measuring information we cannot report verbally. In this method, participants are shown a list of words, such as garden, playground, house, etc. And then they are shown parts of these words like gar, pla, ho, along with parts of other words they had not seen. Now, participants will guess the seen words more quickly. When asked, participants often tell that they are unaware of this and they have only guessed.

Working Memory

A multi-component view of Short-Term Memory (STM) was proposed by Baddeley (1986) who suggested that the STM is not a passive storehouse but rather a work bench that holds a variety of memory materials that are constantly handled, manipulated and transformed as people perform various cognitive tasks. This work bench is called **working memory**. The various components of working memory are as follows

- First component is the phonological (related to speech sounds) loop which holds a limited number of sounds and unless rehearsed they decay within 2 seconds.
- Second component is visuospatial (visual perception of spatial relations) sketchpad which stores visual and spatial information and like phonological loop the capacity of the sketchpad too is limited.
- Third component which Baddeley calls the Central Executive, organises information from phonological loop, visuospatial sketchpad as well as from the LTM. Like a true executive, it allocates attentional resources to be distributed to various informations needed to perform a given cognitive operation and monitors, plans and controls behaviour.

Levels of Processing

In 1972, **Craik** and **Lockhart** proposed the idea of levels of processing. This theory says that the deeper levels of analysis produce more elaborate, long-lasting and stronger memory traces than shallow level analysis. These levels are described as follows

(*i*) **Shallow Level** Information can be analysed in its physical or structural features. For example, one might attend only to the shape of letters in a word (e.g. cat) inspite of whether the word is written in capital or small letters or the colour of the ink in which it is written. This is the first and the shallowest level of processing.

(*ii*) **Intermediate Level** At an intermediate level, one might consider and attend to the phonetic (pronunciation) sounds that are attached to the letters and therefore the structural features are transformed into at least one meaningful word (e.g. cat that has three specific letters). Analysing information at these two levels produces memory that is weak and is likely to decay rather quickly.

(*iii*) **Deepest Level** The third level is deepest at which information is processed. It is retained for a longer period. In order to retain information for longer period, information should be understood in terms of its meaning.

For example, if we imagine cat as an animal with four legs, fur, a tail and invoke an image of a cat and connect that image with our experiences, then word 'cat' will be retained for longer period of time.

Understanding memory as a result of the manner in which information is encoded initially has an important feature of learning. This view of memory will help to realize that while we are learning a new lesson, we must focus on elaborating the meaning of its contents in more detail and must not depend on rote memorisation.

Memory as a Constructive Process

Initially, memory was considered as reproduction of stored materials. Scholars like Ebbinghaus and his followers stressed about the quantity of information that can be stored in the memory and calculated its accuracy by matching the contents of storage and reproduction. If there was any difference in the reproduced material compared to stored material, then it was considered error and a case of memory failure.

This storage metaphor of memory implied that the memory was a passive occurrence of learnt material that has been transported to its long-term storehouse. Another scholar named Bartlett challenged this theory and saw memory as a constructive and not a reproductive process.

He used texts, folk tales, fables, etc and tried to understand the manner in which content of any specific memory gets affected by a person's knowledge, goals, motivation, preferences and various other psychological processes. He conducted simple experiments in which reading of such stumulus materials was followed by fifteen minutes break and then the participants of his experiment recalled what they had read.

Bartlett used the method of **serial reproduction**[3]. In this participants recalled the memory materials repeatedly at different time intervals. While engaging in serial reproduction of learned material, his participants committed a wide variety of errors which Bartlett considered useful in understanding the process of memory construction.

His participants altered the texts to make them more consistent with their knowledge, glossed over the unnecessary details, elaborated the main theme and transformed the material to look more coherent and rational.

Forgetting : Nature and Causes

Forgetting is a common problem among all of us which we experience very frequently. The first proper attempt to understand the nature of forgetting was made by **Hermann Ebbinghaus**. He memorised lists of nonsense syllables and then measured the number of trials he took to relearn the same list at different time intervals.

He used a graph to show the pattern of forgetting.

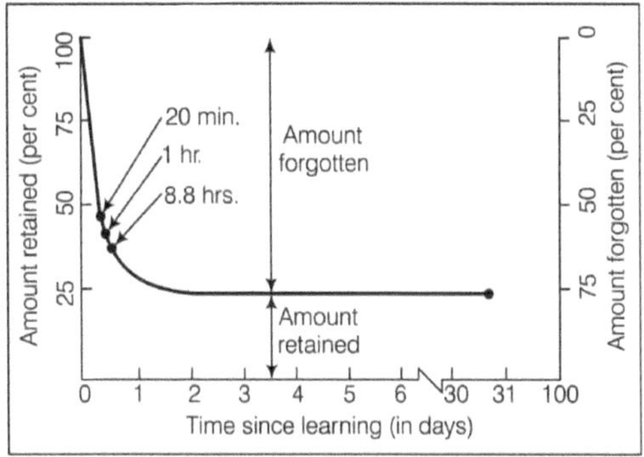

Ebbinghaus's Curve of Forgetting

As the figure shows, the rate of forgetting is maximum in the first nine hours, especially during the first hour. After that the rate
slows down and not much is forgotten even after many days.

Although Ebbinghaus's experiments constituted initial explorations and were not very sophisticated yet they have influenced memory research in many important ways. It is now a well accepted fact that there is always a sharp drop in memory and thereafter the decline is very gradual.

The various causes of forgetting are as follows

Forgetting due to Trace Decay

Trace decay is also called **disuse theory,** which was earliest theory on forgetting. It is assumed that memory leads to modification in the central nervous system, which is similar to physical changes in the brain called **memory traces**. When these memory traces are not used for long time, they fade away and become unavailable.

---

3 **Serial Reproduction** It refers to the method to study memory. In this method, participants of experiment have to recall the same material over different intervals of time.

This theory failed on many grounds. If memory traces decay due to disuse, then people who go to sleep after memorising should forget more than those who remain awake. It is because there is no way in which memory traces can be put to use during sleep. But results show just the opposite i.e people who remain awake after memorising show greater forgetting than those who sleep.

Forgetting due to Interference

Interference theory has been the most influential theory which suggests that forgetting is due to interference between different informations that the memory store contains. It is assumed that learning and memorising involve forming associations between items.

Once associations are formed, they remain intact in the memory. People get many number of such associations and each stays independently without any mutual conflict. Interference comes during the time of retrieval, when these different sets of associations compete with one another for retrieval.

This interference process can be understood with the help of an exercise. For example, request your friend to learn two separate lists of nonsense syllables (list A and list B) one after the other and after a while ask her/him to recall the non-sense syllables of list A. If while trying to recall the items of list A, she/he recalls some of the items of list B, it is because of the association formed while learning list B are interfering with the earlier association which were formed while learning list A.

Types of Interference

There are two kinds of interferences which result in forgetting. It can be **proactive** (forward moving) i.e. what you have learnt earlier interferes with the recall of your immediate learning. It can also be **retroactive** (backward moving) i.e. difficulty in recalling what you have learnt earlier because of learning new material.

In simpler words, in proactive interference, past learninginterferes with the recall of newer learning while in retroactive interference, the newer learning interferes with the recall of past learning.

For example, if a person knows English and she/he finds it difficult to learn French, it is because of proactive interference and if, on the other hand, she/he cannot recall English equivalents of French words that she/he is currently memorising, then it is an example of retroactive interference.

Experimental Designs for Retroactive and Proactive Interference

Retroactive Interference	Phase 1	Phase 2	Testing phase
Experimental Participant/Group	Learns A	Learns B	Recalls A
Control Participant/Group	Learns A	Rests	Recalls A
Proactive Interference			
Experimental Participant/Group	Learns A	Learns B	Recalls B
Control Participant/Group	Rests	Learns B	Recalls B

Forgetting due to Retrieval Failure

Forgetting can also occur because at the time of recall, either the retrieval cues are absent or they are not suitable. Retrieval cues are aids/cues which help us in recovering information stored in the memory. Tulving and his associates carried out several experiments to show that contents of memory may become inaccessible either due to absence or unsuitability of retrieval cues that are available/employed at the time of recall.

Repressed Memories

A traumatic (deeply disturbing) experience emotionally hurts a person. **Sigmund Freud** put forward his view that such experiences are repressed (restrained or oppressed) into the unconscious and are not available for retrieval from memory. It is a kind of repression–painful, threatening, and embarrassing (ashamed) memories are held out of consciousness.

Traumatic experiences may cause psychological amnesia in some persons. Amnesia means the selective overlooking or ignoring events or acts that are not favourable or useful to one's purpose or position. When some individual experience crisis in life, they are completely incapable of coping with such events.

They just close their eyes, ears and mind to such harsh realities of life and take mental flight (i.e. instance of running away) from them. It results in highly generalised amnesia. One of the results of such flights is the emergence of a disorder known as **fugue state**[4]. Persons who become victims of such a state assume a new identity, name, address etc. They have two personalities and one knows nothing about the other.

Forgetfulness under stress and high anxiety is not uncommon. Many hard working and ambitious students aspire for high scores in examination. They study for long hours. But when they receive the question paper, they become extremely nervous and forget everything they have already prepared.

Enhancing Memory

There are a number of strategies and methods for improving memory called **mnemonics**[5]. Some of them involve using images and other lay importance on organisation or arranging learned information by oneself.

---

4 **Fugue State** Persons who become victims of such a state assume a new identity, name, address, etc. They have two personalities and one knows nothing about the other.

5 **Mnemonics** It is a memory technique to help your brain better encode and recall important information.

Mnemonics Using Images

It suggests to create images which are interacting and bring out powerful feelings and clarity in mind, around the material or information you wish to remember. The two famous mnemonic devices, which make interesting use of images are

(i) **The Keyword Method** In this method, we associate a keyword with the information we need to remember. For instance, if we want to learn words of any foreign language. In the keyword method, an English word that sounds similar to the word of a foreign language is identified.

This English word will act as a keyword. For example, if you want to remember the Spanish word for duck which is 'Pato', you may choose 'pot' as the keyword and then evoke images of keyword and the target word (the Spanish word you want to remember) and imagine them as interacting.

You might, in this case, imagine a duck in a pot full of water. This method of learning words of a foreign language is much superior compared to any kind of rote memorisation.

(ii) **The Method of Loci** In this method, items we want to remember are kept as objects arranged in a physical space in the form of visual images. For example, if we want to remember breads, eggs, tomatoes and soap on our way to the market, we may visualise a loaf of bread and eggs placed in our kitchen, tomatoes kept on a table and soap in the bathroom. So when we enter the market we need to do the mental walk from the kitchen to the bathroom for recalling all the items in the list.

This method is useful in remembering items in a serial order. In this method, we first visualise objects/places in a specific sequence and imagine the objects we want to remember and pair them one by one to the physical locations.

Mnemonics Using Organisation

Organisation is like arranging material which you want to remember in a particular order. Some of the methods of organisation are

(i) **Chunking** It refers to mainly grouping together. This method helps in increasing capacity of Short-Term Memory. In chunking, smaller units are combined to form large chunks. Some organisation/arranging principles should be identified in linking smaller units. This will help retrieve the information very easily.

(ii) **First Letter Technique** In this method, you need to pick up first letter of each word you want to remember and arrange them to form another word or a sentence. For example, VIBGYOR (Violet, Indigo, Blue, Green, Yellow, Orange and Red) which are colours of a rainbow are remembered using this method.

Other Approach to Memory Improvement

Mnemonic strategies for memory improvement are so simple and sometimes underestimate complexities of memory tasks and difficulties that people experience while memorising. Instead of mnemonics, a more larger and wide ranging approach to memory improvement has been suggested by many psychologists. Some of these suggestions are

(i) **Deep Level Processing** Craik and Lockhart showed that processing information in terms of meaning that they carry helps us to have better memory.

Deep processing involves asking as many questions related to the information as possible like knowing its meaning, looking at its relation- ships to the facts you already know. In this way, the new information will become a part of your existing knowledge framework and there is an increased probability that it will be remembered.

(ii) **Minimise Interference** Interference is a major cause for forgetting and avoiding it would help our memory. Maximum interference occurs when very similar materials are learned in an order. So, study should be arranged in a manner that you do not learn similar subjects one after the other.

(iii) **Enough Retrieval Cues** Identify the retrieval cues in your study material and link parts of the study material to these cues.

Cues will be easier to remember compared to the entire material. The links you have created between cues and the content will help in the retrieval the information. **Thomas** and **Robinson** have developed a method called PQRST to help students remembering more. It stands for **Preview, Question, Read, Self-recitation** and **Test**.

- Preview refers to having a quick look at the chapter and knowing about its contents.
- Question means raising questions and seeking answers from the lesson.
- Read and look for answers of questions you have raised.
- Self-recitation means try to rewrite what you have read.
- Finally, test yourself how much you have been able to understand.

There is no one method that can solve all problems related to memory and its improvement. In order to improve memory, we need to attend a number of things, like our health status, interest and motivation, familiarily with the subject matter etc. We must learn useful strategies to improve our memory.

Chapter Practice

Objective Questions

• Multiple Choice Questions

1. Which one of them is not a component of working memory given by Baddeley?
   (a) The central executive   (b) Phonological loop
   (c) Control Processes   (d) Visuospatial sketchpad

Ans. (c) Control Processes is not a component of working memory given by Baddeley.

   Baddeley gave three components of working memory, which include, the phonological loop, the central executive, and Visuospatial sketchpad.

2. Who proposed the levels of processing model?
   (a) Atkinson and Shiffrin
   (b) Baddeley
   (c) Craik and Lockhart
   (d) Allan Collins and Ross Quillian

Ans. (c) The levels of processing model was proposed by Craik and Lockhart in 1972.

3. Which of the following is the method used for memory measurement?
   (a) Priming
   (b) Sentence Verification Task
   (c) Free Recall and Recognition
   (d) All of the above

Ans. (d) Free recall and recognition, sentence verification task and priming methods are used for memory measurement.

4. Which of these stages of the memory process are in correct order?
   (a) Encoding, retrieval, storage
   (b) Storage, retrieval, and encoding
   (c) Retrieval, storage, and encoding
   (d) Encoding, storage, and retrieval

Ans. (d) Encoding is the first stage of memory, storage is the second stage of memory and retrieval is the third stage of memory. Thus, the correct answer is (d).

5. The first model of memory, known as the ________. It was proposed by Atkinson and Shiffrin in 1968.
   (a) Levels of processing model
   (b) Stage model
   (c) Dual coding hypothesis
   (d) Working memory model

Ans. (b) The first model of memory is known as the Stage model. It is proposed by Atkinson and Shiffrin in 1968. As per this model, information passes through three memory stores namely, sensory memory, short-term memory and long-term memory.

6. ________ rehearsal simply maintains information through repetition and when such repetitions discontinue the information is lost.
   (a) Elaborative   (b) Practice
   (c) Maintenance   (d) Memory

Ans. (c) Maintenance rehearsal involves repetition of the information for as long as it is needed. When the information is no longer needed or practiced, it fades away.

7. Sigmund Freud was of the view that memories which were too painful, embarrassing and threatening, get ________ into the unconscious to protect the person from feeling difficult emotions.
   (a) stored   (b) suppressed
   (c) repressed   (d) forgotten

Ans. (c) Sigmund Freud was of the view that memories which were too painful, embarrassing and threatening get repressed. Repression is an unconscious process in which difficult memories of the past are involuntarily repressed into the unconscious.

8. The capacity of short-term memory can be increased using ________.
   (a) amnesia   (b) chunking
   (c) meditation   (d) method of loci

Ans. (b) The capacity of short-term memory can be increased using chunking. Chunking is a process by which individual pieces of an information set are broken down and then grouped together in a meaningful whole.

9. Which of these statements about long-term memory is/are correct?

(i) Episodic memory contains memories relating to our personal life experiences.

(ii) One major classification within long-term memory is that of episodic and semantic.

(iii) Implicit memory is a kind of memory that a person is not aware of.

(iv) Procedural memory is the memory of general awareness and knowledge.

Options

(a) (i) & (iv)   (b) (ii) & (iii)   (c) (i) & (iii)   (d) (iii) & (iv)

Ans. (c) Episodic memory contains memories relating to the personal biographical instances from a person's life. Implicit memory contains memories and experiences which are outside our conscious awareness. Thus, option (c) is the correct answer.

10. Which of these are the correct causes of forgetting?

(i) Forgetting due to lack of practice

(ii) Forgetting due to Trace Decay

(iii) Forgetting due to accident

(iv) Forgetting due to Interference

Choose the correct option

(a) (i) & (iii) (b) (ii) & (iii)   (c) (ii) & (iv)   (d) (iii) & (iv)

Ans. (c) The correct causes of forgetting are forgetting due to trace decay and forgetting due to interference.

11. Which of these is not a mnemonic device ?

(i) Rote learning   (ii) The keyword method

(iii) The method of loci   (iv) Schema

Choose the correct option

(a) (i) & (iii)   (b) (ii) & (iii)   (c) (ii) & (iv)   (d) (iii) & (iv)

Ans. (c) The keyword method and the method of loci are not a mnemonic devices.

12. Priyanka learned how to make tea from her father when she was just eight years old. Now, she is twenty three, she makes tea every day for herself without even thinking about it in an effortless manner. This example demonstrates which type of long-term memory?

(a) Episodic memory   (b) Autobiographical memory

(c) Declarative memory   (d) Procedural memory

Ans. (d) This example demonstrates procedural memory type of long-term memory. Procedural memory refers to implicit memories relating to procedures for accomplishing various tasks and skills. Such as making tea or swimming.

13. Nachiket is 18-year-old and is talking to a friend about their childhood. He realises that he does not remember events which occurred before the age of 4 years. This phenomenon is known as __________.

(a) traumatic amnesia   (b) childhood amnesia

(c) repression   (d) forgetfulness

Ans. (b) This phenomenon is known as Childhood amnesia. It is a phenomenon in which people find it difficult or impossible to remember memories from age before 4 or 5.

14. Aditi, who is a 28-year-old singer, suddenly decides to move to a different city. She starts calling herself by the name Smriti and applies for a job as a business accountant. She completely leaves behind her life as Aditi and does not even remember it. Her problem is known as __________.

(a) amnesia   (b) memory disorder

(c) identity crisis   (d) fugue state

Ans. (d) Aditi's problem is known as fugue state. Some people may experience a fugue state which often results from past traumatic experience. In order to mentally escape them, people unconsciously discard their present identity and assume a totally different personality, and may move to a different place altogether.

• Assertion-Reasoning MCQs

Directions (Q. Nos. 1-4) *Each of these questions contains two statements, Assertion (A) and Reason (R). Each of these questions also has four alternative choices, any one of which is the correct answer. You have to select one of the codes (a), (b), (c) and (d) given below.*

(a) Both A and R are true and R is the correct explanation of A

(b) Both A and R are true, but R is not the correct explanation of A

(c) Both A and R are false

(d) A is false and R is true

1. Assertion (A) Information that enters the short-term memory store fades away quickly if not rehearsed.

Reason (R) The short-term memory store has a capacity to hold new information for as long as thirty seconds before it is forgotten.

Ans. (a) Short-term memory is the second system of memory after sensory memory. It has slightly more space to retain information as compared to the sensory memory but less than that of the long-term memory. Thus, Both A and R are true and R is the correct explanation of A.

2. Assertion (A) Simply repeating a piece of information can ensure that it gets stored in the long-term memory.

Reason (R) Elaborative rehearsal involves deep level processing which is important for long-term retention of that information.

Ans. (d) Simple repeating information (maintenance rehearsal) does not guarantee that it will be stored in long-term memory. Elaborative rehearsal involves associating the new information with already existing information. This leads to deeper processing and long-term retention. Thus, A is false and R is true.

3. **Assertion** (A) Some memories are like photographs taken with a camera. Some instances stay in our memory in the form of a vision or image with vivid details.

Reason (R) This is because human memory is flawless as it can remember each and every detail from birth to death.

Ans. (c) Both A and R are false because memories do exist in the form of images of a particular time/event in one's life. However, human memory is not flawless, as it is prone to decay and declining as one grows old. Also, memories before the age of 4 are hard and sometimes impossible to remember due to childhood amnesia.

4. **Assertion** (A) Forgetting can only occur because the memory traces decay over time and retrieval cues do not play an important role in recall.

Reason (R) Retrieval cues are aids which help us in recovering information stored in the memory.

Ans. (d) Forgetting can occur not only because the memory traces have decayed over time (as suggested by the disuse theory) or because independent sets of stored associations interfere at the time of recall (as suggested by the interference theory) but also because at the time of recall, either the retrieval cues are absent or they are inappropriate. Thus, A is false and R is true.

• Case Based MCQs

1. Read the following and answer the questions that follow.

Scenario 1- You happened to remember a certain event. The memory of the event is very arousing or surprising. The memories of this event are like images frozen in memory and tied to particular places, dates and times.

Scenario 2 -There are no memories reported pertaining to early childhood particularly during the first 4 to 5 years. However, you have observed that there is a dramatic increase in the frequency of memories just after early adulthood, i.e. in your twenties.

Scenario 3 -Your brother is a typist. This means he also knows the particular letters on the keyboard. However, when asked to label it, he cannot correctly label blank keys in a drawing of a keyboard.

(i) Identify the type of memory in scenario 1:
(a) Flashbulb Memory   (b) Autobiographical Memory
(c) Implicit Memory   (d) None of these

Ans. (a) Flashbulb memory is the type of memory given in scenario 1. These are memories of events that are very arousing or surprising.

(ii) Second scenario in given case talks about childhood amnesia, it is a form of
(a) Flashbulb Memory   (b) Autobiographical Memory
(c) Implicit Memory   (d) Childhood Memory

Ans. (b) Autobiographical memory is the type of memory given in scenario 2. Childhood amnesia is the inability to recall autobiographical details and personal memories pertaining to early childhood particularly during the first 4 to 5 years.

(iii) The memories that remain outside the conscious awareness of a person is
(a) Flashbulb memory   (b) Autobiographical Memory
(c) Implicit Memory   (d) Unconscious Memory

Ans. (c) Implicit Memory is the memory that remain outside the conscious awareness of a person. Implicit memory is a kind of memory that a person is not aware of it. It is a memory that is retrieved automatically.

(iv) Implicit memory can be retrieved
(a) Directly   (b) Indirectly
(c) Can never be retrieved   (d) None of these

Ans. (b) Implicit memory is retrieved automatically without intention and effort.

(v) Two statements are given in the question below as Assertion (A) and Reasoning (R). Read the statements and choose the appropriate option.

Assertion (A) Even after going years without swimming, most people are able to swim quite easily.

Reason (R) There are some memories which remain out of conscious awareness and are of automatic nature.

Codes
(a) Both A and R are true and R is the correct explanation of A
(b) Both A and R are true, but R is not the correct explanation of A
(c) A is true, but R is false
(d) A is false, but R is true

Ans. (a) Implicit memory is a kind of memory that a person is not aware of. It is a memory that is retrieved automatically. Typing on the keyboard, or swimming after years are examples of implicit memory. Thus, Both A and R are true and R is the correct explanation of A.

(vi) There is a dramatic increase in the frequency of memories just after early adulthood, i.e. in the twenties. Perhaps __________, novelty and importance of events contribute to it.
(a) severity   (b) emotionality
(c) intensity   (d) time

Ans. (b) The dramatic increase in the frequency of memories after early adulthood, i.e. in the twenties is because emotionality, novelty and importance of events contribute to it.

PART 2

Subjective Questions

• Short Answer (SA) Type Questions

1. What is the meaning of the terms 'encoding', 'storage' and 'retrieval'? **(NCERT)**

Ans. **Encoding** It refers to a process by which information is recorded and registered for the first time so that it becomes usable by our memory system. Whenever an external stimulus impacts on our sensory organs, it generates neural impulse i.e the way nerve cells communicate with one another. These are received in different areas of our brain for further processing. In this stage, incoming information is received and some meaning is derived. Then, it represented in a way so that it can be processed further.
Storage It is a process through which information is retained and held over a period of time.
Retrieval It refers to bringing the stored information to her/his awareness so that it can be used for performing various cognitive tasks like problem solving and decision-making.

2. Explain in detail about working memory and its components.

Ans. A multi-component view of Short-Term Memory (STM) was proposed by Baddeley (1986). He suggested that the STM is not a passive storehouse but rather a work bench that holds a variety of memory materials that are constantly handled, manipulated and transformed as people perform various cognitive tasks. This work bench is called working memory. In other words, it is a cognitive system with a limited capacity that can hold information temporarily.

The various components of working memory are as follows

- First component is the phonological (related to speech sounds) loop which holds a limited number of sounds and unless rehearsed they decay within 2 seconds.
- Second component is visuospatial (visual perception of spatial relations) sketchpad which stores visual and spatial information and like phonological loop the capacity of the sketchpad too is limited.
- Third component which Baddeley calls the Central Executive, organises information from phonological loop, visuospatial sketchpad as well as from the Long-Term Memory. Like a true executive, it allocates attentional resources to be distributed to various informations needed to perform a given cognitive operation and monitors, plans and controls behaviour.

3. Discuss about deepest level of processing.

Ans. Craik and Lockhart proposed the idea of levels of processing. The third level in this model is deepest and if information is processed here, it is retained for a longer period. In order to retain information for longer period, information should be understood in terms of its meaning.

For example, if we imagine cat as an animal with four legs, fur, a tail and invoke an image of a cat and connect that image with our experiences, then word cat will be retained for longer period of time.

It implies that, analysing information in terms of its structural and phonetic features will be regarded as shallower processing while encoding in terms of meaning it carries is the deepest processing level that leads to memory that resists forgetting largely.

4. Differentiate between declarative and procedural memories.

Ans. Differences between declarative and procedural memories are as follows

Declarative Memories	Procedural Memory
All information related to facts, names, dates, like sun rises in East, cricket player's names, birth dates of your friends, 15th August, 1947, the day India got independent, etc are part of declarative memory.	It refers to memories relating to procedures for achieving different tasks and skills like how to ride a bicycle, play football, etc.
Facts stored in the declarative memory can described using verbal descriptions.	Contents of procedural memory cannot be described easily. For instance, we can describe how a game of cricket is played but if someone asks how do you ride a bicycle, it is difficult to describe.

5. What is trace decay? What is a major shortcoming of this theory?

Ans. Trace decay is also called disuse theory, which is the earliest theory on forgetting. It is assumed that memory leads to modification in the central nervous system, which is similar to physical changes in the brain called memory traces. When we do not use these memory traces for long time, they simply fade away and become unavailable.

This theory is inadequate on many grounds. (For instance if this theory is true, then people who go to sleep after memorising should forget more than those who remain awake, because memory traces decay due to disuse. But results, show just the opposite i.e. people who remain awake after memorising show greater forgetting than those who sleep.)

6. What is the role of traumatic experiences in developing fugue state in a person?

Ans. Traumatic experiences may cause psychological amnesia in some persons. Amnesia means the selective overlooking or ignoring events or acts that are not favourable or useful to one's purpose or position. When some individual experience crisis in life, they are completely incapable of coping with such events.

They just close their eyes, ears and mind to such harsh realities of life and take mental flight (i.e. instance of running away) from them. It results in highly generalised amnesia.

One of the results of such flights is the emergence of a disorder known as 'fugue state'. Persons who become victims of such a state assume a new identity, name, address, etc. They have two personalities and one knows nothing about the other.

7. How are maintenance rehearsals different from elaborative rehearsals?

Ans. The difference between maintenance rehearsal and elaborative rehearsal is given in the table below

Elaborative rehearsals	Maintenance rehearsals
The rehearsal attempts to connect the 'to be retained information' to the already existing information in long-term memory.	These kinds of rehearsals simply maintain information through repetition and when such repetitions discontinue the information is lost.
From the STM, information enters the long-term memory through elaborative rehearsals.	Short-term memory sets into motion another control process of maintenance rehearsal to retain the information for as much time as required.
For example, the task of remembering the meaning of the word 'humanity' will be easier if the meaning of concepts such as 'compassion', 'truth' and 'benevolence' are already in place.	An example of maintenance rehearsal is repeating the digits of a phone number until we dial them.

8. Discuss the levels of processing propsed by Craik and Lockhart.

Ans. **Craik** and **Lockhart** proposed the idea of levels of processing in 1972. This theory says that the deeper levels of analysis produce more elaborate, long-lasting and stronger memory traces than shallow level analysis.

These levels are described as follows

(i) **Shallow Level** Information can be analysed in its physical or structural features. For example, one might attend only to the shape of letters in a word (e.g. cat) inspite of whether the word is written in capital or small letters or the colour of the ink in which it is written. This is the first and the shallowest level of processing.

(ii) **Intermediate Level** At an intermediate level, one might consider and attend to the phonetic (pronunciation) sounds that are attached to the letters and therefore the structural features are transformed into at least one meaningful word (e.g. cat that has three specific letters). Analysing information at these two levels produces memory that is weak and is likely to decay rather quickly.

(iii) **Deepest Level** The third level is deepest at which information is processed. It is retained for a longer period. In order to retain information for longer period, information should be understood in terms of its meaning.

9. What are the various methods of memory measurement? Discuss any two.

Ans. Free recall and recognition, sentence verification task and priming methods are used for memory measurement. Two methods used for memory measurement are given below

Free Recall and Recognition In free recall method, participants are given some words and are asked to memorise and recall them in any order. The more they are able to recall, the better their memory becomes. In recognition, participants see the items that they had memorised along with distracter items (those that they had not seen) and their task is to identify which one of those they had learnt. The more the number of recognition of old items, the better is the memory.

Priming It is used for measuring information we cannot report verbally. In this method, participants are shown a list of words, such as garden, playground, house, etc. And then they are shown parts of these words like gar, pla, ho, along with parts of other words they had not seen. Now participants will guess the seen words more quickly. When asked, participants often tell that they are unaware of this and they have only guessed.

10. Whenever Pooja sees the pictures of the celebration of her 10th Birthday, she can remember everything in a minute in detail. Explain the type of memory Pooja has.

Ans. The type of memory Pooja has is known as *Flashbulb Memories*. These memories are very detailed. They are like a photo taken with an advanced model camera.

Flashbulb memories are like images frozen in memory and tied to particular places, dates and times. People put in greater effort in the formation of these memories.

Here flashbulb memories are frozen in Pooja's mind with the particular place of the celebrations, timings of it and the friends who attended the party etc. in detail. Thus, whenever she sees the picture, after one minute the recreation of the scene starts in her mind.

11. "Some individuals undergo experiences that are traumatic." How does trauma affect memory? Explain.

Ans. A traumatic experience emotionally hurts a person. Sigmund Freud believed that such experiences are repressed into the unconscious and are not available for retrieval from memory. It is a kind of repression i.e. painful, threatening and embarrassing memories which are held out of consciousness.

In some persons, traumatic experiences may give rise to psychological amnesia. Some individual experiences crisis and are utterly incapable of coping with such events. They close their eyes, ears and minds to such harsh reality of life, and make mental flight from them. It results in highly generalised amnesia. One of the results of such flight is emerging of a disorder known as fugue state. Persons who become victims of such a state have two personalities and one knows nothing about the other.

12. Yash is a student of class 12th. He adopts the method of PQRST for his preparation. Explain the method in detail.

Ans. Yash adopts the method of PQRST which helps him to remember easily. This method stands for preview, question, read, self-recitation and test. The PQRST acronyms mean:

- Preview refers to having quick look at the chapter and knowing about its contents. First Yash follows this step.
- Question means raising questions and seeking answers from the lesson. Yash seeks the probable answers from the lesson.
- He himseft read and look for answers of question that he has raised.
- Self-recitation means try to rewrite what Yash has already read.
- At the end Yash tests himself how much he has understood the chapter.

• Long Answer (LA) Type Questions

1. How is information processed through sensory, short-term and long-term memory, systems?

Ans. Information processed through sensory, short-term and long-term memory systems are discussed as follows

Sensory Memory It has large capacity but is of very short duration i.e. less than a second. The incoming information first enters sensory memory. It registers information from each of the senses with reasonable accuracy.

This system is referred as sensory memories or sensory registers, because informations from all the senses are registered here as exact copy of the stimulus.

For example, seeing visual after-images i.e. the trial of light that stays after the bulb is switched off and hearing reverberations of a sound after the sound has stopped. These are iconic (visual) or echoic (auditory) sensory registers.

Short-Term Memory (STM) Information to which attention is payed enters the second memory store called the Short-term Memory (STM). It holds small amount of information for a brief period of time (usually for 30 seconds or less). Atkinson and Shiffrin proposed that information in STM is usually encoded in terms of sound and unless practised continuously, it may get lost from the STM in less than 30 seconds.

Long-Term Memory (LTM) Information that survive the capacity and duration limitations of STM finally enter the Long-term Memory. It is a permanent storehouse of all informations that may be very recent incidents or very distant events that might happened 10 years back. It has been shown that once any information enters LTM, it is never forgotten. The reason for this is that information gets encoded logically or meaningfully i.e. in terms of the meaning that any information carries.

2. Explain Hermann Ebbinghaus's curve of forgetting and also interference theory on forgetting?

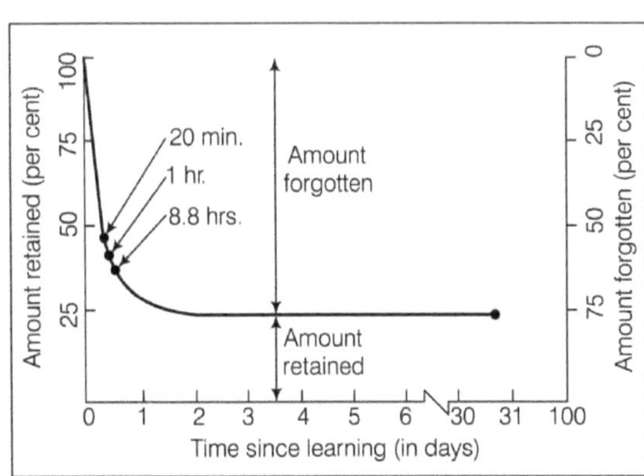

Ans. **Hermann Ebbinghaus' Curve of Forgetting** The first proper attempt to understand the nature of forgetting was made by Hermann Ebbinghaus. He memorised lists of nonsense syllables and then measured the number of trials he took to relearn the same list at different time intervals. He used a graph to show the pattern of forgetting which is given above

In the above graph, one can observe that the rate of forgetting is maximum in the first 9 hours in general and first 1 hour in particular. Later, the rate slows down and not much is forgotten even after many days.

Though this research was very simple, it influenced memory research. As of now, it is accepted by all that memory drops sharply and thereafter the decline is gradual.

Forgetting Due to Interference

Interference theory has been the most influential theory which suggests that forgetting is due to interference between different informations that the memory store contains. It is assumed that learning and memorising involve forming associations between items.

Once associations are formed, they remain intact in the memory. People get many number of such associations and each stays independently without any mutual conflict.

Interference comes during the time of retrieval, when these different sets of associations compete with one another for retrieval.

3. "Mnemonic strategies for memory improvement are too simple and sometimes underestimate complexities of memory tasks and difficulties people experience while memorising." Discuss other methods of memory improvement which are more effective.

Ans. Mnemonic strategies can be simplistic in nature and can sometimes fail to be effective in more comprehensive memory tasks. In place of mnemonics, a more comprehensive approach to memory improvement has been suggested by many psychologists. In such an approach, emphasis is laid on applying knowledge about memory processes to the task of memory improvement. Some of these suggestions are as follows

(a) **Engage in Deep Level Processing** Deep processing would involve asking as many questions related to the information as possible, considering its meaning and examining its relationships to the facts you already know. In this way, the new information will become a part of your existing knowledge framework and the chances that it will be remembered are increased. Processing information in terms of meaning that they convey leads to better memory.

(b) **Minimise Interference** Minimise interference is caused when very similar materials are learned in a sequence. To avoid these students can arrange their study in such a way that they do not learn similar subjects one after the other. Instead, pick up some other subjects unrelated to the previous one. If that is not possible, distribute the learning/practice. This means giving oneself intermittent rest periods while studying to minimise interference.

(c) **Using Sufficient Retrieval Cues :** While learning something, one should identify retrieval cues inherent in the study material. Then link parts of the study material to these cues. Cues will be easier to remember compared to the entire content and the links you have created between cues and the content will facilitate the retrieval process.

4. Give memories as a constructive process.

Ans. Memory was considered as reproduction of stored materials. Scholars like Ebbinghaus and his followers stressed about the quantity of information that can be stored in the memory and calculated its accuracy by matching the contents of storage and reproduction. If there was any difference in the reproduced material compared to stored material, then it was considered error and a case of memory failure.

This storage metaphor of memory implied that the memory was a passive occurrence of learnt material that has been transported to its long-term storehouse. Another scholar named Bartlett challenged this theory and saw memory as a constructive and not a reproductive process.

He used texts, folk tales, fables, etc and tried to understand the manner in which content of any specific memory gets affected by a person's knowledge, goals, motivation, preferences and various other psychological processes. He conducted simple experiments in which reading of such stumulus materials was followed by fifteen minutes break and then the participants of his experiment recalled what they had read.

Bartlett used the method of **serial reproduction**. In this participants recalled the memory materials repeatedly at different time intervals. While engaging in serial reproduction of learned material, his participants committed a wide variety of errors which Bartlett considered useful in understanding the process of memory construction.

His participants altered the texts to make them more consistent with their knowledge, glossed over the unnecessary details, elaborated the main theme and transformed the material to look more coherent and rational.

5. Define mnemonics and other memory enhancing strategies.

Ans. There are a number of strategies and methods for improving memory called mnemonics. Some of them involve using images and other lay importance of organisation or arranging learned information by oneself.

Mnemonics using Images It suggests to create images which are interacting and bring out powerful feelings and clarity in mind, around the material or information which is wish to remember.

The two famous mnemonic devices, which make interesting use of images are as follows

(i) **The Keyword Method** In this method, we associate a keyword with the information we need to remember. For instance, if we want to learn words of any foreign language an English word that sounds similar to the word of a foreign language is identified. This English word will act as a keyword.

This method of learning words of a foreign language is much superior compared to any kind of rote memorisation.

(ii) **The Method of Loci** In this method, items we want to remember are kept as objects arranged in a physical space in the form of visual images. This method is useful in remembering items in a serial order. In this method, we first visualise objects/places in a specific sequence and imagine the objects we want to remember and pair them one by one to the physical locations.

Mnemonics using Organisation Organisation is like arranging material which you want to remember in a particular order. Some of the methods of organisation are

(i) **Chunking** It refers to mainly grouping together. This method helps in increasing capacity of STM. In chunking, smaller units are combined to form large chunks. Some organisation/arranging principles should be identified in linking smaller units. This will help retrieve the information very easily.

(ii) **First Letter Technique** In this method, you need to pick up first letter of each word you want to remember and arrange them to form another word or a sentence. For example, VIBGYOR (Violet, Indigo, Blue, Green, Yellow, Orange and Red) which are colours of a rainbow are remembered using this method.

• Case Based Questions

1. Read the case given below and answer the following questions.

A 55 year old mother and her two daughters are sitting together and discussing some concerns their mother has. She feels that she has become very forgetful off-late. She sometimes finds it hard to recall some words while conversing, or sometimes she forgets the hotel she stayed in on her first college trip. At times, she even forgets grocery items she wanted to buy when she is out in the market.

Her three daughters try to identify the cause of her forgetfulness. The first daughter suggests that it is an age related decline. She says that sometimes information decays from memory if it is not used or practised.

Her second daughter believes that forgetfulness is a result of inability to access retrieval cues, or having no cues at the time of recall. When we do not have the aid to remember or recall something, it causes forgetfulness.

(i) Identify the causes of forgetfulness explained by the first and the second daughter in the case?

Ans. The first daughter believes that forgetting is caused by trace decay. It states that memory leads to modification in the central nervous system, which causes physical changes in the brain called memory traces. When these memory traces are not used for a long time, they simply fade away and become unavailable.

The second daughter is of the view that forgetting is due to retricval failure. This theory believes that the contents of memory may become inaccessible either due to absence or inappropriateness of retrieval cues that are available/employed at the time of recall.

(ii) Which psychologist made the first attempt to understand the nature of forgetting?

Ans. The first systematic attempt to understand the nature of forgetting was made by Hermann Ebbinghaus through experiments. Ebbinghaus's experiments constituted initial explorations and they influenced memory research in many important ways.

(iii) What is the third cause of forgetting which is not demonstrated in the given passage?

Ans. The third cause of forgetting is interference. It states that forgetting is due to interference between various information that the memory store contains. When new information interferes with the recall of old information or vice versa, interference is the cause of forgetfulness.

2. Read the case given below and answer the following questions.

A psychology teacher wants to demonstrate how new information is processed and the factors which help in long-term retaining of that information. He gives an example and says that one might attend only to the shape of letters in a word, for instance, ball- inspite of whether the word is written in capital or small letters or the colour of the ink in which it is written.

Then, one might consider and attend to the phonetic sounds that are attached to the letters and therefore the structural features are transformed into at least one meaningful word say, a word ball that has four specific letters.

However, there is a third level at which information can be processed. For instance, you may think of a ball as a toy that is round, bounces, can be in multiple colours, and is used in various sports. He suggests that each student should visualize an image of a ball and connect that image with their own unique experiences.

(i) Identify the theory mentioned in the case. Who was the proponent of the theory?

Ans. The levels of processing view, was proposed by Craik and Lockhart in 1972. According to this, whether or not some new information will be remembered for a long time, is dependent on how deeply and on how many levels it is processed.

(ii) As per the model, identify the first and intermediate levels of processing in the above case?

Ans. Shallow level processing in this case is simply attending only to the shape of letters in a word ball. At intermediate level, one might attend to the phonetic sounds that are attached to the letters and therefore the structural features are transformed into at least one meaningful word say, a word ball that has four specific letters.

(iii) Which action, in this case, demonstrates the deep level processing? Why is deep level processing important?

Ans. For example, in deep level processing, a person would process/analyse information on various levels, such as considering its meaning & examining its relationship to previously learned facts. In deeper level processing, one may think of a ball as a toy that is round, bounces, can be in multiple colours, and is used in various sports. This process is important in order to ensure that the information is retained for a longer period, that it gets analysed and understood in terms of its meaning.

Chapter Test

Multiple Choice Questions

1. Which of the following is defined as overlapping or disturbance of different memory traces on each other?

    (a) Forgetting   (b) Conditioning

    (c) Interference   (d) Recall

2. What is defined as the temporary or long-term loss of material that was learnt earlier?

    (a) Forgetting   (b) Memory

    (c) Perception   (d) None of these

3. In order to ensure that the information is retained for a longer period, it is important that it is understood in terms of its______.

    (a) traits   (b) meaning

    (c) usage   (d) complexity

4. From the short-term memory, information enters the long-term memory through ______.

    (a) Retrieval cues   (b) Maintenance rehearsal

    (c) Elaborative rehearsal   (d) Mnemonics

Short Answer (SA) Type Questions

5. Define memory. List its stages.

6. Who gave stage model? List different memory systems present in stage model.

7. Define chunking with an example.

8. Why is third component of working memory called executive?

9. Define implicit memory with an example.

10. What do you mean by cognitive economy?

11. What are proactive and retroactive interferences?

12. Discuss briefly about sensory memory.

13. Write about deepest level of processing.

14. What is fugue state? How does it develop?

15. Describe the functioning of PQRST method.

Long Answer (LA) Type Questions

16. 'Memory is a constructive process'. Discuss.

17. Discuss various methods of memory improvement which are more effective than mnemonics in detail.

Answers

1. (c)   *2.* (a)   *3.* (b)   *4.* (c)

Practice Paper 1*
(Solved)

General Instructions

■ Time : **2 Hours**
■ Max. Marks : **35**

1. There are 9 questions in the question paper. All questions are compulsory.
2. Question no. 1 is a Case Based Question, which has five MCQs. Each question carries one mark.
3. Question no. 2-6 are Short Type Questions. Each question carries 3 marks.
4. Question no. 7-9 are Long Answer Type Questions. Each question carries 5 marks.
5. There is no overall choice. However, internal choice have been provided in some questions.
   Students have to attempt only on of the alternatives in such questions

** As exact Blue-print and Pattern for CBSE Term II exams is not released yet. So the pattern of this paper is designed by the author on the basis of trend of past CBSE Papers. Students are advised not to consider the pattern of this paper as official. It is just for practice purpose.*

Case Based Questions

1. Read the given passage and answer the following questions. $(1 \times 5 = 5)$

The parents of Ankur, a 7-year-old boy, take him to the family practitioner because they have become increasingly concerned about his behaviour not only in school but also at home. In the first grade, he has been bored, disruptive, fighting with classmates, and rude to his teacher. At home he cannot sit still and meals have been very unpleasant. The lad himself wonders why he is there. The parents have 2 older daughters who say their brother is a "pain" and spoiled. There were no pregnancy or birth problems and the child is on no medications. The doctor decides more information is required before any treatment is indicated. She wants careful observations of the child both at home and in school. On observing the child for a certain period, she identified that the child does not follow instructions, has difficulty in getting along with parents, and is negatively viewed by his peers. He also had difficulties in reading or learning basic subjects in schools in spite of the fact that there is no deficit in his intelligence.

(i) Identify the disorder that the child is having
   (a) Attention Deficit Hyperactivity Disorder (ADHD)   (b) Post-Traumatic Stress Disorder (PTSD)
   (c) Seasonal affective disorder   (d) Dissociative disorder

(ii) On the basis of observation, which of the following is/are characteristics of this disorder?
   (a) Impulsivity   (b) Excessive motor activity
   (c) An inability to attend   (d) All of these

(iii) Identify the incorrect statement with respect to this disorder.
   (a) This is a very common behavioural disorder found among children of the primary school age.
   (b) The disorder is more prevalent among girls than among boys.
   (c) There is no concrete evidence for a biological basis of the disorder.
   (d) Social-psychological factors (e.g., home environment, family pathology) have been found to account for this disorder.

  (iv) Which of the following methods can be used to treat this disorder?
     (a) Use of drug called Ritalin   (b) Behavioural management programs
     (c) Cognitive behavioural training   (d) All of these
  (v) __________ factors (e.g., home environment, family pathology) have been found to account for ADHD more reliably than other factors.
     (a) cognitive   (b) socio-psychological
     (c) emotional   (d) biological

Short Answer Questions $(3 \times 5 = 15)$

2. Describe the interference theory of forgetting. (3)

Or Mnemonic memory strategies can sometimes be too simplistic and unhelpful in more complex memory tasks. What are three ways by which memory can be improved?

3. Define learning disability and describe any two of its symptoms. (3)

Or What is an unconditioned stimulus and describe the different types of unconditioned stimuli.

4. Write a short note on properties of attentional processes. (3)

Or Write a short note on divided attention.

5. Sanya watches her elder brother Rishabh play cricket with his friends. Then, she starts imitating his brother and asks him to let her play with him. She also eats the same ice-cream her brother likes. Describe this method of learning. (3)

6. Briefly explain selective attention and the Filter theory. (3)

Long Answer Questions $(5 \times 3 = 15)$

7. Explain the determinants of classical conditioning. (5)

Or Explain the difference between operant and classical conditioning?

8. It is important to remember that the biological, cognitive, and socio-emotional processes are interwoven. These processes influence changes in the development of the individual as a whole throughout the human life-span. Based on this, explain the assumptions of Life-Span Perspective (LSP). (5)

Or Development does not take place in a vacuum. Transition during one's lifetime such as entering school, becoming an adolescent, finding jobs, marrying, having children, retirement, etc., all are joint functions of the biological changes and changes in one's environment. The environment can change or alter during any time of the individual's lifespan. Identify and explain this theoretical view of development.

9. Describe the Atkinson and Shiffrin Model for processing memory. (5)

Or Radhika was telling her friend how she is able to recall certain historical facts accurately and how she has become effortlessly good at cycling over a period of time. Which memory system is responsible for the tasks Radhika is able to perform and explain its subtypes?

Answers

1. (i) (*a*) The child is having Attention Deficit Hyperactivity Disorder (ADHD).

  (ii) (*d*) The basis of observation all of the given options are the characteristics of ADHD.

  (iii) (*b*) The disorder is more prevalent among girls than among boys is the incorrect statement about ADHD.

  (v) (*b*) Socio-psychological factors have been found to account for ADHD more reliable than other factors.

2. Interference theory which suggests that forgetting is due to interference between various information that the memory store contains. This theory assumes that learning and memorising involve forming of associations between items and once acquired, these associations remain intact in the memory.

There are two kinds of interferences that may result in forgetting. Interference can be proactive (forward moving) which means what you have learnt earlier interferes with the recall of your subsequent learning or retroactive (backward moving) which refers to difficulty in recalling what you have learnt earlier because of learning a new material.

For example, if you know English and you find it difficult to learn French, it is because of proactive interference and if, on the other hand, you cannot recall English equivalents of French words that you are currently memorising, then it is an example of retroactive interference.

Or

A more comprehensive approach to memory improvement has been suggested by many psychologist in place of mnemocis. Such approaches can be as follows

(a) **Engage in Deep Level Processing** Deep processing would involve asking as many questions related to the information as possible, considering its meaning and examining its relationships to the facts you already know. In this way, the new information will become a part of your existing knowledge framework and the chances that it will be remembered are increased.

(b) **Minimise Interference** Interference is a major cause of forgetting and therefore one should try to avoid it as much as possible. Arranging study in such a way that one does not learn similar subjects one after the other. If that is not possible, distribute learning/practice.

(c) **Give Yourself enough Retrieval Cues** Cues are easier to remember compared to the entire content and the links one creates between cues and the content will facilitate the retrieval process.

3. Learning disability is a general term. It refers to a heterogeneous group of disorders manifested in terms of difficulty in the acquisition of learning, reading, writing, speaking, reasoning, and mathematical activities. Learning disabilities may be observed as a distinct handicapping condition in children of average to superior intelligence, adequate sensory motor systems, and adequate learning opportunities.

There are many symptoms of learning disabilities. Two symptoms of learning disability are

(i) Learning-disabled children have poor motor coordination and poor manual dexterity. This is evident in their lack of balance, inability to sharpen pencil, handle doorknobs, difficulty in learning to ride a bicycle, etc.

(ii) Learning-disabled children have disorders of attention. They get easily distracted and cannot sustain attention on one point for long. More often than not, attentional deficiency leads to hyperactivity, i.e. they are always moving, doing different things, trying to manipulate things incessantly.

Or

An unconditioned stimulus(US) is the one which elicits or evokes a natural/ true response or behaviour. A few examples of US include, removing our hand from an extremely hot utensil, or fragrance of food can trigger feelings of hunger naturally.

It is a component of classical conditioning. The unconditioned stimuli used in studies of classical conditioning are basically of two types, i.e. appetitive and aversive.

Appetitive unconditioned stimuli automatically elicit approach responses, such as eating, drinking, caressing, etc. These responses give satisfaction and pleasure. On the other hand, aversive US, such as noise, bitter taste, electric shock, painful injections, etc., are painful, harmful, and elicit avoidance and escape responses. It has been found that appetitive classical conditioning is slower and requires a greater number of acquisition trials, but aversive classical conditioning is established in one, two or three trials depending on the intensity of the aversive US.

4. The process through which certain stimuli are selected from a group of others is generally referred to as attention. For example, when you enter your classroom you encounter several things in it, such as doors, walls, windows, paintings on walls, tables, chairs, students, schoolbags, water bottles, and so on, but you selectively focus only on one or two of them at one time.

The various properties of attention are

(i) Attention also refers to several other properties like alertness, concentration and search.

Alertness refers to an individual's readiness to deal with stimuli that appear before her/him.

Concentration refers to focusing of awareness on certain specific objects while excluding others for the moment. All these activities require some kinds of effort on the part of people. Attention in this sense refers to "effort allocation".

(ii) Attention has a focus as well as a fringe. When the field of awareness is centered on a particular object or event, it is called focus or the focal point of attention. On the contrary, when the objects or events are away from the center of awareness and one is only vaguely aware of them, they are said to be at the fringe of attention.

(iii) Attention has been classified in a number of ways. A process-oriented view divides it into two types, namely selective and sustained.

Or

Sometimes we can also attend to two different things at the same time. When this happens, it is called divided attention. In day-to-day life, we attend to several things at the same time. For example, people driving a car and talking to a friend, or attending to phone calls on a mobile set, or putting on sunglasses, or listening to music. If we watch them closely, we will notice that they are still allocating more effort to driving than to other activities, even though some attention is given to other activities.

It indicates that on certain occasions attention can be allocated to more than one thing at the same time. However, this becomes possible only with highly practiced activities, because they become almost automatic and require less attention to perform than new or slightly practiced activities.

Automatic processing has three main characteristics; (i) It occurs without intention, (ii) It takes place unconsciously, and (iii) It involves very little (or no) thought processes (e.g., we can read words or tie our shoelaces without giving any thought to these activities).

5. In the given instance, Sanya is learning new behaviours through the observational method of learning. In this kind of learning, human beings learn social behaviours, therefore, it is sometimes called social learning.

In observational learning observers acquire knowledge by observing the model's behaviour, but performance is influenced by the model's behaviour being rewarded or punished.

In many situations individuals do not know how to behave. They observe others and emulate their behaviour. This form of learning is called modeling.

An example of this type of learning can involve observing superiors and likeable persons and then emulating their behaviour in a novel social situation is a common experience.

It has also been shown that children learn and develop various personality characteristics through observational learning. Aggressiveness, prosocial behaviour, courtesy, politeness, diligence, and indolence are acquired by this method of learning.

6. Selective attention is concerned mainly with the selection of a limited number of stimuli from a large number of stimuli. Selective attention is the process of focusing on a particular thing in the environment for a specific period of time.This means that it can deal only with a few stimuli at a given moment of time .A number of theories have been developed to explain the process of selective attention. One of the major theories of selective attention is the Filter theory.

Filter theory was developed by Broadbent (1956). According to this theory, many stimuli simultaneously enter our receptors creating a kind of "bottleneck" situation. Moving through the short-term memory system, they enter the selective filter, which allows only one stimulus to pass through for higher levels of processing. Other stimuli are screened out at that moment of time. Thus, we become aware of only that stimulus, which gets access through the selective filter.

7. Classical conditioning is a form of associative learning. It is based on the Stimulus–Stimulus (S-S) learning approach in which one stimulus becomes a signal for another stimulus.

The following are the determinants of classical conditioning

1. **Time Relations between Stimuli** The classical conditioning procedures, are basically of four types based on the time relations between the onset of conditioned stimulus (CS) and unconditioned stimulus (US). The first three are called forward conditioning procedures, and the fourth one is called backward conditioning procedure.

   The basic experimental arrangements of these procedures are as follows

   (a) When the CS and US are presented together, it is called simultaneous conditioning.

   (b) In delayed conditioning, the onset of CS precedes the onset of US. The CS ends before the end of the US.

   (c) In trace conditioning, the onset and end of the CS precedes the onset of US with some time gap between the two.

   (d) In backward conditioning, the US precedes the onset of CS.

2. **Type of Unconditioned Stimuli** The unconditioned stimuli used in studies of classical conditioning are basically of two types, i.e. appetitive and aversive. Appetitive unconditioned stimuli automatically elicit approach responses, such as eating, drinking, caressing, etc. On the other hand, aversive US, such as noise, bitter taste, electric shock, painful injections, etc., are painful, harmful and elicit avoidance and escape responses.

3. **Intensity of Conditioned Stimuli** This influences the course of both appetitive and aversive classical conditioning. More intense conditioned stimuli are more effective in accelerating the acquisition of conditioned responses. It means that the more intense the conditioned stimulus, the fewer are the number of acquisition trials needed for conditioning.

Or

The difference between classical conditioning and operant conditioning are as follows

Classical Conditioning	Operant Conditioning
Classical conditioning is a process in which learning is possible by forming association between two stimuli.	Operant Conditioning, refers to the learning in which the organism studies the relation between responses and its consequences.
It Focuses on involuntary, automatic behaviour.	It involves applying reinforcement or punishment after a behavior
It is based on Involuntary or reflexive behavior.	It is based on Voluntary behavior.
It responses under control of stimulus	It responses under control of organism.
Conditioned and Unconditioned stimulus are well defined.	Conditioned stimulus is not defined.
Occurrence of unconditioned stimulus controlled by experimenter.	Occurrence of unconditioned stimulus controlled by organism.

8. The study of development according to the Life-Span Perspective (LSP) includes the following assumptions

- Development is lifelong, i.e. it takes place across all age groups starting from conception to old age. It includes both gains and losses, which interact in dynamic (change in one aspect goes with changes in others) ways throughout the life-span.

- The various processes of human development, i.e. biological, cognitive, and socio-emotional are interwoven in the development of a person throughout the life-span.

- Development is multi-directional. Some dimensions or components of a given dimension of development may increase, while others show decrement. For example, the experiences of adults may make them wiser and guide their decisions. However, with an increase in age, one's performance is likely to decrease on tasks requiring speed, such as running.

- Development is highly plastic, i.e. within a person, modifiability is found in psychological development, though plasticity varies among individuals. This means skills and abilities can be improved or developed throughout the life-span.

- Development is influenced by historical conditions. For example, the experiences of 20-year old who lived through the freedom struggle in India would be very different from the experiences of 20-year old today.

- Development is the concern of a number of disciplines. Different disciplines like psychology, anthropology, sociology, and neuro-sciences study human development, each trying to provide answers to development throughout the life-span.

- An individual responds and acts on contexts, which include what was inherited, the physical environment, social, historical, and cultural contexts. For example, the life events in everyone's life are not the same, such as, death of a parent, accident, earthquake, etc., affect the course of one's life as also the positive.

Or

The passage is based on Urie Bronfenbrenner's contextual view of development which emphasises the role of environmental factors in the development of an individual.

According to this theory, a person's environment consists of the following systems which affect their development

- The microsystem is the immediate environment/setting in which the individual lives. It is in these settings where the child directly interacts with social agents – the family, peers, teachers and neighbourhood.

- The mesosystem consists of relations between these contexts. For instance, how a child's parents relate to the teachers, or how the parents view the adolescent's friends, are experiences likely to influence an individual's relationships with others.

- The exosystem includes events in social settings where the child does not participate directly, but they influence the child's experiences in the immediate context. For example, the transfer of father or mother may cause tension among the parents which might affect their interactions with the child or the general amenities available to the child like quality of schooling, libraries, medical care, means of entertainment, etc.

- Macrosystem includes the culture in which the individual lives.

- Chronosystem involves events in the individual's life course, and socio-historical circumstances of the time such as, divorce of parents or parents' economic setback, and their effect on the child. In a nutshell, Bronfenbrenner's view is that a child's development is significantly affected by the complex world that envelops her/him– whether it be the minutiae of the conversations s/he has with her/his playmates, or the social and economic life circumstances into which s/he is born.

9. Atkinson and Shiffrin in 1968. It is known as the Stage Model. According to the Stage Model, there are three memory systems : the Sensory Memory, the Short-term Memory and the Long-term Memory. Each of these systems have different features and perform different functions with respect to the sensory inputs.

Sensory Memory The incoming information first enters the sensory memory. Sensory memory has a large capacity. However, it is of very short duration, i.e. less than a second. It is a memory system that registers information from each of the senses with reasonable accuracy. Often this system is referred to as sensory memories or sensory registers because information from all the senses are registered here as exact replica of the stimulus.

Short-term Memory You will perhaps agree that we do not attend to all the information that impinge on our senses. Information that is attended to enter the second memory store called the short-term memory (abbreviated as STM), which holds a small amount of information for a brief period of time (usually for 30 seconds or less). Atkinson and Shiffrin propose that information in STM is primarily encoded acoustically, i.e. in terms of sound and unless rehearsed continuously, it may get lost from the STM in less than 30 seconds.

Long-term Memory Materials that survive the capacity and duration limitations of the STM finally enter the long-term memory (abbreviated as LTM) which has a vast capacity. It is a permanent storehouse of all information that may be as recent as what you ate for breakfast yesterday to as distant as how you celebrated your sixth birthday. It has been shown that once any information enters the long-term memory store it is never forgotten because it gets encoded semantically, i.e. in terms of the meaning that any information carries.

Or

Radhika's example is an example of Long-term memory (LTM) which has a vast capacity and is known as a permanent storehouse of all information. It may involve what someone ate for breakfast two days ago to as distant as how they celebrated their eighth birthday.

One major classification within the LTM is that of Declarative and Procedural (sometimes called non-declarative) memories. All information pertaining to facts, names, dates, such as a rickshaw has three wheels or that India became independent on 15th August, 1947 or a frog is an amphibian or you and your friend share the same name, are part of declarative memory.

On the other hand, procedural memory refers to memories relating to procedures for accomplishing various tasks and skills such as how to ride a bicycle, how to make tea or play basketball.

Tulving has proposed yet another classification and has suggested that the declarative memory can either be Episodic or Semantic. Episodic memory contains biographical details of our lives. Memories relating to our personal life experiences constitute the episodic memory and it is for this reason that its contents are generally emotional in nature. For example, the memory of the first time a girl scored the highest mark in her class.

Semantic memory, on the other hand, is the memory of general awareness and knowledge. All concepts, ideas and rules of logic are stored in semantic memory. For instance, it is because of semantic memory that we remember the meaning of say 'non-violence' or remember that $2+6=8$.

Practice Paper 2*
(Unsolved)

General Instructions

- Time : **2 Hours**
- Max. Marks : **35**

1. There are 9 questions in the question paper. All questions are compulsory.
2. Question no. 1 is a Case Based Question, which has five MCQs. Each question carries one mark.
3. Question no. 2-6 are Short Type Questions. Each question carries 3 marks.
4. Question no. 7-9 are Long Answer Type Questions. Each question carries 5 marks.
5. There is no overall choice. However, internal choice have been provided in some questions.
   Students have to attempt only on of the alternatives in such questions

** As exact Blue-print and Pattern for CBSE Term II exams is not released yet. So the pattern of this paper is designed by the author on the basis of trend of past CBSE Papers. Students are advised not to consider the pattern of this paper as official. It is just for practice purpose.*

Case Based Questions

1. Read the given passage and answer the following questions. $(1 \times 5 = 5)$

Charles is an adolescent and he is the younger brother of Maria. Their parents have a dysfunctional and abusive relationship. Charles goes out of home to escape the fights and falls into the bad company of some delinquents and Maria wants to protect him from them. To make him realize the seriousness of the situation. Maria told him about Delinquency and its bad effects. She explains that delinquency is a socially unacceptable behaviour, legal offences, criminal acts, and so on. Its examples are truancy, running away from home, stealing or burglary or acts of vandalism. Adolescents with delinquency and behavioural problems tend to have a negative self-identity, decreased trust and a low level of achievement. Any young person whose conduct is characterised by antisocial behaviour that is beyond parental control and subject to legal action is known as Juvenile delinquent (below 16 years of age for boys and 18 years for girls). The juveniles who commit a crime also suffer the effects as they may lose their freedom while being placed on probation. They may lose ground academically as well. Sometimes their repetitive criminal actions lead them into jail like an adult. The delinquency may even have future consequences on the adolescent's college and career choices. However, most delinquent children do not remain delinquent forever.

(i) Which of the following constitutes a type of juvenile delinquency?

(a) Status offense   (b) Civil offense   (c) Criminal offense   (d) Both (a) and (c)

(ii) Many child development experts, psychologists, sociologists, and criminologists, agree that the child's ________ often exercises the greatest influence on his/her early life.

(a) friends   (b) family   (c) teachers   (d) religious leaders

(iii) Existing studies of juvenile delinquents have shown that

(a) children who have been abused are more likely to become involved in delinquent behaviour.
(b) children who have been abused are equally as likely to become involved in delinquent behaviour as children that were not abused.
(c) children who have been abused are less likely to become involved in delinquent behaviour.
(d) there is no correlation between juvenile delinquency and children who have been abused.

(iv) Consider the following statements and determine if they are correct.
   1. Delinquency is often associated with low parental support, inappropriate discipline, and family discord.
   2. Eloping from home, stealing or burglary or acts of vandalism are examples of delinquancy.
   (a) Both are correct   (b) Only 1 is correct   (c) Only 2 is correct   (d) Both are incorrect

(v) Which of the following will not help Charles to make good and healthy choices ?
   (a) Change in their peer group, becoming more aware of their social responsibilities
   (b) Developing feelings of self worth, imitating positive behaviour of the role models.
   (c) Breaking negative attitudes, and overcoming poor self-concept help in reduction of delinquent behaviour.
   (d) Making friends with children who are homeless and delinquents

Short Answer Questions $(3 \times 5 = 15)$

2. All the 9th and 10th standard students of a school were invited to a seminar on health and well-being. In that seminar the speaker says that adolescence is marked by the beginning of puberty or sexual maturity. Describe the physical changes which occur during adoloscence.   (3)

Or A group of friends was debating on whether cricket is a man's game or woman's game or both or woman's activity or a man's. Based on this define gender roles and sex roles. Additionally, briefly explain how gender roles are formed.

3. Explain how continuous or partial reinforcement facilitates learning?   (3)

Or Describe the determinants of verbal learning?

4. Memory is conceptualised as a process consisting of three independent, though interrelated stages. Identify and explain these three stages of memory.   (3)

Or Several experiments have been conducted to test the accuracy of the stage model. Describe the different results which have been produced through these research studies.

5. Define and explain 'span of attention'.   (3)

6. There are certain types of cues which are often used by artists to induce depth in two dimensional paintings. They are also known as pictorial cues. Based on this, identify the type of depth perception cues and describe any three of its subtypes.   (3)

Long Answer Questions $(5 \times 3 = 15)$

7. A four-year-old boy was walking home one night with his parents. While walking, he screamed and exclaimed that he saw a ghost with many hands. He had mistaken a big tree with many branches for a ghost. This instance confirms that perception can be inaccurate at times. Based on this instance, identify the phenomena and describe its subtypes.   (5)

Or A psychology professor teaching perception, states that human beings are not just mechanical and passive recipients of stimuli from the external world. They are creative beings, and try to understand the external world in their own ways. Based on this, explain the different factors which play an important role in giving meaning to the external world.

8. A mother praises her daughter every time she cleans her room, or throws waste material in the garbage bin. The girl feels encouraged to continue maintaining cleanliness wherever she goes. Based on this instance, identify and describe the type of conditioning. Explain its different subtypes.   (5)

Or A teacher notices that a student in her 9th standard class has trouble in reading and writing, fails to solve basic mathematical problems, shows clumsiness, finds it hard to tell time and also has poor motor coordination. Identify the problem being faced by the student and describe it in detail.

9. Describe the different methods of memory measurement.   (5)

Or Describe the levels of processing view with examples.

Answers

1.   *(i) (a)*   *(ii) (b)*   *(iii) (a)*   *(iv) (a)*   *(v) (d)*

Practice Paper 3*

(Unsolved)

General Instructions

1. There are 9 questions in the question paper. All questions are compulsory.
2. Question no. 1 is a Case Based Question, which has five MCQs. Each question carries one mark.
3. Question no. 2-6 are Short Type Questions. Each question carries 3 marks.
4. Question no. 7-9 are Long Answer Type Questions. Each question carries 5 marks.
5. There is no overall choice. However, internal choice have been provided in some questions.
   Students have to attempt only one of the alternatives in such questions

■ Time : **2 Hours**
■ Max. Marks : **35**

** As exact Blue-print and Pattern for CBSE Term II exams is not released yet, so the pattern of this paper is designed by the author on the basis of trend of past CBSE Papers. Students are advised not to consider the pattern of this paper as official. It is just for practice purpose.*

Case Based Questions

1. Read the given passage and answer the following question.   (1 × 5 = 5)

In an experiment, participants were asked to watch a film clipping of an event (a car accident). Then the group of participants was divided into two groups. Both the groups were asked some questions. One of the questions was "how fast were the cars going when they smashed into each other". In another question the verb smashed was replaced with the verb 'contacted'.

The participants belonging to the group who were asked the first question (which included the word 'smashed') estimated the speed of the cars as 40.8 kmph. However, those who were asked the second question (i.e. with the word 'contacted') estimated that the speed of the cars was only 31.8 kmph.

(i) Identify the kind of memory being demonstrated in the above case?
   (a) Eyewitness Memory
   (b) False Memory
   (c) Forced Memory
   (d) Both (a) and (b)

(ii) In the above case, questions asked interfere with the
   (a) Source
   (b) Channel
   (c) Feedback
   (d) Encoding of the event

(iii) What do you think, what led to the difference in answer among two groups.
   (a) Film Clipping
   (b) Nature of the Question
   (c) Depends on the Participants
   (d) Can't be determined

(iv) Two statements are given in the question below as Assertion (A) and Reasoning (R). Read the statements and choose the appropriate option.

Assertion (A) Sometimes people's recollection of an event can be manipulated or influenced.

Reason (R) The nature of leading questions can alter the memory.

Options

(a) Both A and R are true, and R is the correct explanation of A
(b) Both A and R are true, but R is not the correct explanation of A
(c) A is true, R is false
(d) A is false, R is true

(v) What can cause the eyewitnesses to get overwhelmed and not pay attention to details while encoding?

(a) The face of the perpetrator   (b) Crowd or mob
(c) Tragedy and violence   (d) None of these

Short Answer Questions $(3 \times 5 = 15)$

2. Define and describe implicit memory. (3)

Or Explain Bartlet's view on constructive memory.

3. A class teacher wanted to assess the student's memory ability. He decides to give them a list of verbal items/words to see how they memorise and recall the list. In this instance, which method of studying verbal learning is being applied? Describe an additional method of verbal learning? (3)

Or Sanjeev compared his initial days of learning the guitar to the present. He notices that his skills have greatly improved and now he is able to play the guitar very effortlessly as compared to the early days of learning. Based on this instance, explain skill acquisition and the phases of skill acquisition?

4. Describe the bobo doll experiment and what was its conclusion? (3)

Or Describe how motivation and preparedness for learning facilitate/influence learning?

5. Write a short note on the socio-cultural influences on perception. (3)

6. Define selective attention and explain the multimode theory of selective attention? (3)

Long Answer Questions $(5 \times 3 = 15)$

7. Explain the three major theories of selective attention. (5)

Or Describe the nature and varieties of stimulus?

8. Describe the stage of infancy in detail? (5)

Or Describe genes and environment influence development?

9. Whenever a man comes home wearing a cap, he takes his son to the park to play. So, whenever his son sees the man come home wearing a cap, he gets instantly happy because he has associated the cap with a trip to the park. Identify and describe this type of conditioning? (5)

Or Mani takes his younger sister Avantika on his bicycle to school every day. Avantika learns the route from their home to the school through her brother but since she has never ridden the bicycle herself she has not demonstrated that she learnt the route to school. One day when her brother is on leave, she has to ride the bicycle to the school alone. She follows the same route that her brother would have taken to the school. She had created a mental map of the route. What type of learning does this instance demonstrate? Explain it in detail.

Answers

1.   *(i) (a)*   *(ii) (d)*   *(iii) (b)*   *(iv) (a)*   *(v) (c)*

Printed by Libri Plureos GmbH in Hamburg,
Germany

9 789325 796867